An Introduction to English Phonology

An Introduction to English Phonology

April McMahon

OXFORD

UNIVERSITY PRESS

Oxford University Press

Oxford   New York
Athens   Auckland   Bangkok   Bogotá   Buenos Aires   Calcutta
Cape Town   Chennai   Dar es Salaam   Delhi   Florence   Hong Kong   Istanbul
Karachi   Kuala Lumpur   Madrid   Melbourne   Mexico City   Mumbai
Nairobi   Paris   São Paulo   Singapore   Taipei   Tokyo   Toronto   Warsaw

and associated companies in

Berlin   Ibadan

Published by Oxford University Press, Inc.
198 Madison Avenue, New York, New York 10016
by arrangement with Edinburgh University Press Ltd
22 George Square, Edinburgh, United Kingdom

Oxford is a registered trademark of Oxford University Press, Inc.

Library of Congress Cataloging-in-Publication Data Available

ISBN 0-19-521890-6 hardcover
ISBN 0-19-521891-4 paperback

Typeset in Janson by Norman Tilley Graphics
Printed and bound in Great Britain by
MPG Books Ltd, Bodmin, Cornwall

Contents

To colleagues

This textbook is designed for use on ten- or twelve-week introductory courses on English phonology of the sort taught in the first year of many English Language and Linguistics degrees, in British and American universities. Students on such courses can struggle with phonetics and phonology; it is sometimes difficult to see past the new symbols and terminology, and the apparent assumption that we can immediately become consciously aware of movements of the vocal organs which we have been making almost automatically for the last eighteen or more years. This book attempts to show students why we need to know about phonetics and phonology, if we are interested in language and our knowledge of it, as well as introducing the main units and concepts we require to describe speech sounds accurately.

The structure of the book is slightly unusual: most textbooks for beginning students, even if they focus on English, tend to begin with an outline of elementary universal phonetics, and introduce phonological concepts later. I have started the other way round: in a book which is primarily intended as an introduction to phonology, it seems appropriate to begin with one of the major units of phonology, the phoneme. The idea of phonological contrast is a complex but necessary one, and students do seem, at least in my experience, to cope well with an introduction of this more abstract idea before they become embroiled in the details of phonetic consonant and vowel classification. When it comes to presenting those details, I have also chosen to use verbal descriptions rather than diagrams and pictures in most cases. There are two reasons for this. First, students need to learn to use their own intuitions, and this is helped by encouraging them to introspect and think about their own vocal organs, rather than seeing disembodied pictures of structures which don't seem to belong to them at all. Secondly, I know from meeting fellow-sufferers that I am not the only person to find supposedly helpful cartoons and diagrams almost impossible to decipher, and to feel that the right word can be worth a thousand pictures. If students or teachers feel the visual centres of their brains are being insufficiently stimulated, many diagrams and photographs are available in the additional reading recommended at the end of each chapter.

In a textbook of this length, choices are also inevitable: mine are to concentrate on segmental phonology, with some discussion of stress and syllables, but a brief mention only of intonation. The theoretical machinery introduced extends only to segments, features, basic syllabification and elementary realisation rules: issues of morphophonemics and rules versus constraints are again mentioned only briefly. My hope is that a thorough grounding in the basics will help students approach more abstract theoretical and metatheoretical issues in more advanced courses with greater understanding of what the theories intend to do and to achieve, and with more chance of evaluating competing models realistically.

My warmest thanks for help and advice on this book go to my students in Sheffield (who were not necessarily aware that I was just as interested in their attitude to exercises and examples as in their answers), and to Heinz Giegerich and Andrew Linn (who were all too aware that their input was required, and have withstood pestering with typical patience). Particular thanks also to my son Aidan, who, following our recent move to Yorkshire, replaced /ʌ/ with /ʊ/ in STRUT words, quite consciously and systematically, during the writing of this book. If a six-year-old can work this out, first-year undergraduates have no excuse.

1 Sounds, spellings and symbols

1.1 Phonetics and phonology

Although our species has the scientific name *Homo sapiens*, 'thinking human', it has often been suggested that an even more appropriate name would be *Homo loquens*, or 'speaking human'. Many species have sound-based signalling systems, and can communicate with other members of the same species on various topics of mutual interest, like approaching danger or where the next meal is coming from. Most humans (leaving aside for now native users of sign languages) also use sounds for linguistic signalling; but the structure of the human vocal organs allows a particularly wide range of sounds to be used, and they are also put together in an extraordinarily sophisticated way.

There are two subdisciplines in linguistics which deal with sound, namely phonetics and phonology, and to fulfil the aim of this book, which is to provide an outline of the sounds of various English accents and how those sounds combine and pattern together, we will need aspects of both. Phonetics provides objective ways of describing and analysing the range of sounds humans use in their languages. More specifically, articulatory phonetics identifies precisely which speech organs and muscles are involved in producing the different sounds of the world's languages. Those sounds are then transmitted from the speaker to the hearer, and acoustic and auditory phonetics focus on the physics of speech as it travels through the air in the form of sound waves, and the effect those waves have on a hearer's ears and brain. It follows that phonetics has strong associations with anatomy, physiology, physics and neurology.

However, although knowing what sounds we can in principle make and use is part of understanding what makes us human, each person grows up learning and speaking only a particular human language or languages, and each language only makes use of a subset of the full range of possible, producible and distinguishable sounds. When we turn to the

1

characteristics of the English sound system that make it specifically English, and different from French or Welsh or Quechua, we move into the domain of phonology, which is the language-specific selection and organisation of sounds to signal meanings. Phonologists are interested in the sound patterns of particular languages, and in what speakers and hearers need to know, and children need to learn, to be speakers of those languages: in that sense, it is close to psychology.

Our phonological knowledge is not something we can necessarily access and talk about in detail: we often have intuitions about language without knowing where they come from, or exactly how to express them. But the knowledge is certainly there. For instance, speakers of English will tend to agree that the word *snil* is a possible but non-existent word, whereas **fnil* is not possible (as the asterisk conventionally shows). In the usual linguistic terms, *snil* is an accidental gap in the vocabulary, while **fnil* is a systematic gap, which results from the rules of the English sound system. However, English speakers are not consciously aware of those rules, and are highly unlikely to tell a linguist asking about those words that the absence of **fnil* reflects the unacceptability of word-initial consonant sequences, or clusters, with [fn-] in English: the more likely answer is that *snil* 'sounds all right' (and if you're lucky, your informant will produce similar words like *sniff* or *snip* to back up her argument), but that **fnil* 'just sounds wrong'. It is the job of the phonologist to express generalisations of this sort in precise terms: after all, just because knowledge is not conscious, this does not mean it is unreal, unimportant or not worth understanding. When you run downstairs, you don't consciously think 'left gluteus maximus, left foot, right arm; right gluteus maximus, right foot, left arm' on each pair of steps. In fact, you're unlikely to make any conscious decisions at all, below the level of wanting to go downstairs in the first place; and relatively few people will know the names of the muscles involved. In fact, becoming consciously aware of the individual activities involved is quite likely to disrupt the overall process: think about what you're doing, and you finish the descent nose-first. All of this is very reminiscent of our everyday use of spoken language. We decide to speak, and what about, but the nuts and bolts of speech production are beyond our conscious reach; and thinking deliberately about what we are saying, and how we are saying it, is likely to cause self-consciousness and hesitation, interrupting the flow of fluent speech rather than improving matters. Both language and mobility (crawling, walking, running downstairs) emerge in developing children by similar combinations of mental and physical maturation, internal abilities, and input from the outside world. As we go along, what we have learned becomes easy, fluent and automatic; we only become dimly aware of what complexity lies behind our actions when we realise we have made a speech error, or see and hear a child struggling to say a word or take a step. Phonologists, like anatomists and physiologists, aim to help us understand the nature of that underlying complexity, and to describe fully and formally what we know in a particular domain, but don't know we know.

The relationship between phonetics and phonology is a complex one, but we might initially approach phonology as narrowed-down phonetics. Quite small babies, in the babbling phase, produce the whole range of possible human sounds, including some which they never hear from parents or siblings: a baby in an English-speaking environment will spontaneously make consonants which are not found in any European language, but are to be found closest to home in an African language, say, or one from the Caucasus. However, that child will then narrow down her range of sounds from the full human complement to only those found in the language(s) she is hearing and learning, and will claim, when later trying to learn at school another language with a different sound inventory, that she cannot possibly produce unfamiliar sounds she made perfectly naturally when only a few months old. Or within a language, subtle mechanical analysis of speech reveals that every utterance of the same word, even by the same speaker, will be a tiny fraction different from every other; yet hearers who share that language will effortlessly identify the same word in each case. In this sense, phonetics supplies an embarrassment of riches, providing much more information than speakers seem to use or need: all those speakers, and every utterance different! Phonology, on the other hand, involves a reduction to the essential information, to what speakers and hearers think they are saying and hearing. The perspective shifts from more units to fewer, from huge variety to relative invariance, from absolutely concrete to relatively abstract; like comparing the particular rose I can see from my window, or roses generally in all their variety (old-fashioned, bushy, briar; scented or not; red, yellow, shocking pink), to The Rose, an almost ideal and abstract category to which we can assign the many different actual variants. A white dog-rose, a huge overblown pink cabbage rose, and a new, genetically engineered variety can all be roses with no contradiction involved. In linguistic terms, it's not just that I say *tomahto* and you say *tomayto*; it's that I say *tomahto* and *tomahto* and *tomahto*, and the three utterances are subtly different, but we both think I said the same thing three times.

1.2 Variation

The discussion so far may suggest a rather straightforward dichotomy: phonetics is universal, while phonology is language-specific. But things are not quite that simple.

First, phonologists also attempt to distinguish those patterns which are characteristic of a single language and simply reflect its history, from others where a more universal motivation is at issue. In the case of the absence of *fnil, or more generally the absence of word-initial [fn-] clusters, we are dealing with a fact of modern English. It is perfectly possible to produce this combination of sounds; there are words in many languages, including Norwegian *fnise* 'giggle', *fnugg* 'speck', which begin with just that cluster; and indeed, it was quite normal in earlier periods of English – *sneeze*, for example, has the Old English ancestor *fnēsan*, while Old English *fnæd* meant 'hem, edge, fringe'; but it is not part of the inventory of sound combinations which English speakers learn and use today. The same goes for other initial clusters, such as [kn-]: this again was common in Old English, as in *cnāwan* 'to know', and survives into Modern English spelling, though it is now simply pronounced [n]; again, [kn-] is also perfectly normal in other languages, including German, where we find *Knabe* 'boy', *Knie* 'knee'.

On the other hand, if you say the words *intemperate* and *incoherent* to yourself as naturally as you can, and concentrate on the first consonant written *n*, you may observe that this signals two different sounds. In *intemperate*, the front of your tongue moves up behind your top front teeth for the *n*, and stays there for the *t*; but in *incoherent*, you are producing the sound usually indicated by *ing* in English spelling, with your tongue raised much further back in the mouth, since that's where it's going for the following [k] (spelled *c*). Processes of assimilation like this involve two sounds close together in a word becoming closer together in terms of pronunciation, making life easier for the speaker by reducing vocal tract gymnastics. Assimilation is an everyday occurrence in every human language; and it is particularly common for nasal sounds, like the ones spelled *n* here, to assimilate to following consonants. Explaining universal tendencies like this one will involve an alliance of phonology and phonetics: so phonologists are interested in universals too.

However, phonological differences also exist below the level of the language: frequently, two people think of themselves as speakers of the same language, but vary in their usage (sometimes you do say *tomayto*, while I say *tomahto*). This is not just an automatic, phonetic matter: in some cases a single speaker will always use one variant, but in others, individuals will use different variants on different occasions. It also has nothing to do with the physical characteristics of the different speakers, or the different environments in which they may find themselves, although this was a common belief in the days before linguists adopted a rigorous scientific methodology: thus, Thomas Low Nichols, a nineteenth-century commentator on American English, speculates that 'I know of no physiological reason why a Yankee should talk through his nose, unless he got in the habit of shutting his mouth to keep out the cold fogs and drizzling north-easters of Massachusetts Bay'. There is a natural tendency for geographically distant accents to become more different; the same tendency has led the various Romance languages, such as Italian, Spanish, Romanian and French, to diverge from their common ancestor, Latin. In addition, speakers often wish, again sub-consciously, to declare their allegiance to a particular area or social group by using the language of that group; these accent differences can be powerful social markers, on which we judge and are judged.

Furthermore, although there are agreed conventions, which form the basis of the phonology of languages and of accents, those conventions can be subverted in various ways, just as is the case for other areas of human behaviour. In short, even phonologically speaking, there is more than one English – indeed, on one level, there are as many Englishes as there are people who say they speak English. Providing an adequate and accurate phonological description is therefore a challenge: on the one hand, a single system for English would be too abstract, and would conceal many meaningful differences between speakers; on the other, a speaker-by-speaker account would be too detailed, and neglect what unifies speakers and allows them to recognise one another as using the same system. In what follows, we will concentrate on a small number of varieties – Southern Standard British English; Scottish Standard English; General American, the most frequently encountered broadcast-ing variety in the United States; and New Zealand English. All of these are abstractions, and combine together a range of constantly shifting subvarieties; but they are useful to illustrate the range of variation within English, and represent groupings recognisable to their speakers, provid-ing a level of accuracy which a monolithic 'English' system could not.

1.3 The International Phonetic Alphabet

So far, the examples given have been rather general ones, or have in-volved analogies from outside language. Giving more detailed examples demands a more specific vocabulary, and a notation system dedicated to the description of sounds. The English spelling system, although it is the system of transcription we are most used to, is both too restrictive and too lenient to do the job.

Without a universal transcription system for phonetics and phonology, writing down the unfamiliar sounds of other languages presents an almost insuperable challenge. Take, for example, a sound which is used only paralinguistically in English (that is, for some purpose outside the language system itself), but which is a perfectly ordinary consonant in other languages, just as [b] in *but* or [l] in *list* are in English, namely the 'tut-tut' sound made to signal disapproval. When we see this, we do not think of a whole word, but of a repeated clicking. This description is hopelessly inadequate, however, for anyone else trying to recognise the sound in question, or learn how to make it. Hearing a native speaker use the 'tut-tut' click in a language where it is an ordinary consonant does not help us understand how the sound is made or how it compares with others. Likewise, adopting the usual spelling from that language (assuming it is not one of the many without an orthography) might let us write the 'tut-tut' sound down; but this technique would not produce a universal system for writing sounds of the world's languages, since linguists would tend to use their own spelling systems as far as possible, and opt for representations from the languages they happened to know for other sounds. There would be little consistency, and generalisation of such a system would be difficult.

The situation is worse with 'exotic' sounds which do not happen to coincide even with those used paralinguistically in English: groping towards a description in ordinary English is far too vague to allow accurate reproduction of the sound in question; and indeed, such sounds tended by early commentators to be regarded as unstable or not quite proper. John Leighton Wilson, who published a brief description of the African language Grebo in 1838, had considerable difficulties with sounds which do not have an obvious English spelling, and tended to resolve this by simply not transcribing them at all. Thus, he notes that 'There is a consonant sound intermediate between b and p, which is omitted ... with the expectation that it will, in the course of time, gradually conform to one or the other of the two sounds to which it seems allied'. Similarly, he observes 'a few words in the language so completely nasal that they cannot be properly spelled by any combination of letters whatever'.

It is for these reasons that the International Phonetic Alphabet was proposed in 1888; it has been under constant review ever since by the International Phonetic Association, and the latest revision dates from 1996. It is true that a certain amount of learning is required to become familiar with the conventions of the IPA and the characteristics of sounds underlying the notation: but once you know that 'tut-tut' is [ǀ], an alveolar click, it will always be possible to produce the relevant sound accurately; to write it down unambiguously; and to recognise it in other languages.

Although a universal system of description and transcription might be desirable in principle, and even in practice when dealing with unfamiliar languages and sounds, readers of a book both in and on English might question the necessity of learning the IPA. However, precisely the same types of problems encountered above also appear in connection with the phonology of English, and some new ones besides.

First, there is considerable ambiguity in the English spelling system, and it works in both directions: many sounds to one spelling, and many spellings to one sound. The former situation results in 'eye-rhymes', or forms which look as if they ought to have the same pronunciation, but don't. There are various doggerel poems about this sort of ambiguity (often written by non-native speakers who have struggled with the system): one begins by pointing out a set of eye-rhymes – 'I gather you already know, Of *plough* and *cough* and *through* and *dough*'. Those four words, which we might expect to rhyme on the basis of the spelling, in fact end in four quite different vowels, and *cough* has a final consonant too. On the other hand, *see, sea, people, amoeba* and *fiend* have the same long [iː] vowel, but five different spellings.

Despite these multiple ambiguities, attempts are regularly made to indicate pronunciations using the spelling system. None are wholly successful, for a variety of different reasons. The lack of precision involved can be particularly frustrating for phonologists trying to discover characteristics of earlier stages of English. John Hart, a well-known sixteenth-century grammarian, gives many descriptions of the pronunciations of his time, but the lack of a standard transcription system hampers him when it comes to one of the major mysteries of English phonology at this period, namely the sound of the vowel spelled *a*. Hart mentions this explicitly, and tells us that it is made 'with wyde opening of the mouthe, as when a man yawneth': but does that mean a back vowel, the sort now found for Southern British English speakers in *father*, or a front one, like the *father* vowel for New Zealanders or Australians? Similarly, Thomas Low Nichols, discussing mid-nineteenth-century American English, notes that 'It is certain that men open their mouths and broaden their speech as they go West, until on the Mississippi they will tell you "thar are heaps of bar [bear] over thar, whar I was raised"'. Here we have two related difficulties: the nature of the *a* vowel, and what the orthographic *r* means, if anything. Most British English speakers (those from Scotland, Northern Ireland and some areas of the West

Country excepted) will pronounce [r] only immediately before a vowel: so a London English speaker would naturally read the quote with [r] at the end of the first *thar*, *bar* and *whar*, but not the second *thar*, where the next word begins with a consonant. However, a Scot would produce [r] in all these words, regardless of the following sound. Which is closer to what Thomas Low Nichols intended? Orthographic *r* is still problematic today: when Michael Bateman, in a newspaper cookery column, writes that 'This cook, too, couldn't pronounce the word. It's not pah-eller; it's pie ey-yar', he is producing a helpful guide for most English English speakers, who will understand that his 'transcription' of *paella* indicates a final vowel, since they would not pronounce [r] in this context in English; but he is quite likely to confuse Scots or Americans, who would pronounce [r] wherever *r* appears in English spelling, and may therefore get the mistaken idea that *paella* has a final [r] in Spanish. In short, the fact that there are many different Englishes, and that each quite properly has its own phonological interpretations of the same spelling system (which, remember, is multiply ambiguous in the first place), means we encounter inevitable difficulties in trying to use spelling to give explicit information about sounds.

The same problems arise in a slightly different context when writers try to adapt the spelling system to indicate accent differences:

> 'Good flight?' asked Jessica at Christchurch Airport. I melodramatically bowed a depressurization-deaf ear towards her ... before answering that it had been a little gruelling.
>
> 'You are a bit pale. But you'll still be able to get breakfast at the hotel ... '
>
> What Jessica actually said was *git brikfist it the hitil.* The Kiwi accent is a vowel-vice voice, in which the *e* is squeezed to an *i*, the *a* elongated to an *ee*. A New Zealander, for example, writes with a *pin*, and signals agreement with the word *yis*.
>
> (Mark Lawson, *The Battle for Room Service: Journeys to all the safe places*, Picador (1994), 22)

Lawson succeeds in showing that a difference exists between New Zealand and English English, and provides a very rough approximation of that difference. However, anyone who has listened to New Zealand speakers will know that their pronunciation of *pen* is not identical to Southern British English *pin*, as Lawson's notation would suggest; and readers who have not encountered the variety might arrive at a number of different interpretations of his comments that New Zealand vowels are 'squeezed' or 'elongated'. The National Centre for English Cultural Tradition in Sheffield has produced a list of local phrases, again rendered in a modified version of English spelling: it includes *intitot* ('Isn't it hot?'), *eez gooinooam* ('he's going home'), and *lerrus gerrus andzwesht* ('Let's get our hands washed'). Sometimes the modifications are obvious; the lack of *h* in *intitot* suggests that no |h| is pronounced, and the substitution of *r* for *t* in *lerrus gerrus* signals the common northern English weakening of [t] to [r] between vowels. But why double *rr*? The double vowel letters in *gooinooam* presumably signal long vowels; but the *rr* in *lerrus* certainly does not mean a long consonant. Such lists are amusing when the reader knows the variety in question; but reading the list in a respectable imitation of an unfamiliar accent would be rather a hit and miss affair.

The same goes for dialect literature, even when there is an informally agreed set of emendations to the spelling system, as is perhaps the case for Scottish English. Tom Leonard's poem 'Unrelated Incidents (3)' begins:

> this is thi
> six a clock
> news thi
> man said n
> thi reason
> a talk wia
> BBC accent
> iz coz yi
> widny wahnt
> mi ti talk
> aboot thi
> trooth wia
> voice lik
> wanna yoo
> scruff.

Again, many of the alterations are entirely transparent for a reader who is familiar with Scottish English – *aboot* does sound like *a-boot* rather than having the diphthong usually found in Southern British English *about*, and *widny* rather than *wouldn't* is both clear and accurate. However, not everything is so obvious. *Trooth* is written to match *aboot*, and the two words do have the same vowel in Scots – but the former is pronounced like its English English equivalent, whereas the latter is not; so we might ask, why alter both? *Thi* is consistently written for *the*, and there is indeed a slight difference in those final vowels between the two varieties; but if we compare Tom Leonard with Mark Lawson, the impression given is that *thi* (= *the*) for a Scot sounds like *pin* (= *pen*) for a New Zealander, which is not the case at all.

In some cases of this type, there are attempts to introduce new symbols into the English spelling system to represent accent differences: one particularly common device is to use an apostrophe. This has become a fairly conventional and familiar device; but again, it turns out to be ambiguous. For instance, take the three phrases *I feel 'ot*, *She was waitin'*, and *Give us the bu'er*. The first is perhaps the most straightforward: many speakers of non-standard varieties of English consistently drop their [h]s (and we all do, in pronouns under low stress, for instance, as in *What did he say?*, where [h] will be pronounced only in extraordinarily careful speech). In this case, then, the apostrophe means the standard [h] is omitted. This might, however, lead us to believe that an apostrophe always means something is missing, relative to the standard pronunciation. Informal characterisations might support this hypothesis, since speakers producing forms like *waitin'* and *bu'er* are frequently described as 'dropping their gs' and 'dropping their ts' (or 'swallowing their ts') respectively: an article in *The Independent* of 28 June 2000 reports that '... the entire cast of *East Enders* ... swallow their ts, ps and ks like true Glasgow speakers when using such words as "sta'ement" and "sea'belt"'. However, the phonetic facts suggest otherwise. Whereas *'ot* simply lacks an initial consonant, *waitin'* does not lack a final one: instead, the final [ŋ] of *waiting* has been replaced by [n] (recall the discussion of *incoherent* versus *intemperate* above). For most speakers, apart from some from the Midlands and north of England, there was no [g] to drop in the first place, simply one nasal in more formal circumstances, which shifts to another nasal in informal conversation. In *bu'er*, we also find one consonant, this time [t], being replaced by another, the glottal stop; but this time, the replacement is only found in English as an alternative for another sound. It has no independent orthographic representation, and is strongly associated with informal, non-standard and stigmatised usage.

If we are to consider these variants objectively, however, we need a system of notation which will allow us to observe them neutrally, providing transcriptions of each variety in its own terms: seeing the glottal stop as IPA [ʔ], which is a perfectly normal consonant in, say, Arabic, rather than regarding it as an unsymbolisable grunt, or a debased form of another consonant, may allow us to analyse the facts of accent variation without seeing every departure from an idealised standard variety as requiring apology. The linguistic arbitrariness but social grounding of such judgements is apparent from forms like *car park* – a standard Southern British English pronunciation will have no [r] in either word, and to a Scottish English speaker with both [r]s invariably produced, there is certainly something missing; but I have not seen this represented as *ca' pa'k*, or heard southerners accused of 'swallowing their [r]s'.

For all these cases, what we need is a consistent, agreed system of transcription, so that we can assess the accent differences we find and compare them with confidence. Of course, no purely phonetic system is going to help with the meaning of items of vocabulary a reader has not met before – an IPA transcription will not tell you what a *bampot* is, or *glaur*, or a *beagie*, if you don't know. But at least you have the comfort of knowing how the natives pronounce it.

At the same time, this is an introductory text on English, and not a handbook of general phonetics, so only those sections of the IPA relevant to English sounds will be considered, beginning with consonants in Chapter 3, and moving on to vowels, where most accent variation in English is concentrated. However, before introducing the IPA in detail, we must also confront a phonological issue. As we have already seen, native speakers of a language cannot always be relied upon to hear every theoretically discernible gradation of sound. In some cases, the IPA supplies alternative symbols in cases where speakers will be quite sure they are hearing the same thing; and this is not a universal limitation of human ears, but rather varies from language to language. To illustrate this, and to resolve the problem that sometimes speakers think they are hearing something quite different from what they objectively are hearing, we must introduce the concept of the phoneme.

Recommendations for reading

Comparisons of human and animal language are provided in Aitchison (1983), and there is relevant discussion in Pinker (1994). Fletcher and MacWhinney (1994) is a collection of papers on aspects of language acquisition. Trudgill (2000) provides an accessible introduction to dialects and why they are important, although it is fairly narrowly focussed on England. A detailed account of the history and usage of the IPA is provided in International Phonetic Association (1999), and further information is available at
http://www.arts.gla.ac.uk/IPA/ipa.html

2 The phoneme: the same but different

2.1 Variation and when to ignore it

Recognising that two objects or concepts are 'the same but different' ought to present a major philosophical problem; the phrase itself seems self-contradictory. However, in practice we categorise elements of our world in just this way on an everyday basis. A two-year-old can grasp the fact that his right shoe and left shoe are very similar, but actually belong on different feet; and as adults, we have no difficulty in recognising that lemons and limes are different but both citrus fruits, or that misery and happiness are different but both emotions. This sort of hierarchical classification is exactly what is at issue when we turn to the notion of the phoneme.

Humans excel at ignoring perceptible differences which are not relevant for particular purposes. To illustrate this, take a piece of paper and write your normal signature six times. There will certainly be minor differences between them, but you will still easily recognise all those six signatures as yours, with the minor modifications only detectable by uncharacteristically close scrutiny. Perhaps more to the point, someone else, checking your signature against the one on your credit card, will also disregard those minor variants, and recognise the general pattern as identifying you. There are exceptions, of course: some alterations are obvious, and usually environmentally controlled, so if someone jolts your elbow, or the paper slips, you apologise and sign again. On the whole, however, the human mind seems to abstract away from irrelevant, automatic variation, and to focus on higher-level patterns; though we are typically unaware of that abstraction, and of the complex processes underlying it. This relatively high tolerance level is why mechanical systems constructed to recognise hand-written or spoken language are still elementary and highly complex, and why they require so much training from each potential user.

2.2 Conditioned variation in written language

Since we are more used to thinking explicitly about written language than about our speech, one way of approaching this issue of abstraction is through our conscious knowledge of the rules of writing. When children learn to write, they have to master the conventions governing the use of capital and lower-case letters. Children often tend to learn to write their name before anything else, and this will have an initial capital; and children are also great generalisers, and indeed over-generalisers; for instance, first words often have a much wider range of meanings than their adult equivalents. Thus, for a one-year-old, *cat* may mean 'any animal' (whether real, toy, or picture), *tractor* 'any vehicle', and *Daddy* 'any male adult'; these broad senses are later progressively narrowed down. It follows that children may at first try to write all words with initial capitals, until they are taught the accepted usage, which in modern English is for capitals to appear on proper names, *I*, and the first word in each sentence, and lower-case letters elsewhere, giving the prescribed patterns in (1).

(1) a. Anna   *annA
      Africa   *africA
   b. An apple for Anna
   c. Give Anna an apple.

Precisely how the capital and lower-case letters are written by an individual is not relevant, as long as they are recognisable and consistently distinct from other letters — *an* needs to be distinguished from *on*, and *An* from *In*, but it does not especially matter whether we find a, *a* or ɑ for lower-case, and A, *A*, A or **A** for capital; it all depends who we copy when we first learn, what our writing instruments and our grip on them are like, or typographically, which of the burgeoning range of fonts we fancy.

Again, we seem readily able to perceive that all these subtly different variants can be grouped into classes. There is a set of lower-case and a set of capital letters, and the rules governing their distribution relate to those classes as units, regardless of the particular form produced on a certain occasion of writing. Moreover, the lower-case and capital sets together belong to a single, higher-order unit: they are all forms, or realisations of 'the letter a', an ideal and abstract unit to which we mentally compare and assign actual written forms. 'The letter a' never itself appears on paper, but it is conceptually real for us as users of the alphabet: this abstract unit is a grapheme, symbolised <a>; triangle brackets are conventionally used for spellings. The choice of symbol is purely conventional: since it is a conceptual unit, and since we do not know what units look like in the brain, we might as well use an arbitrary sign like <§>, or <✪>, or give it a name: <a> is Annie Apple in the children's Letterland series for beginning readers. However, it is convenient to use a form that looks like one of the actual realisations, as this will help us to match up the abstract grapheme with the actual graphs which manifest it in actual writing.

The rules governing the distribution of <a> and other graphemes are not, however, absolute natural laws. Learning that proper names and sentences begin with capitals is appropriate for a child writing modern English, but not for a child learning German, who would need to learn instead that all nouns (not just *Anna* and *Afrika* but also *Apfel* 'apple') always begin with a capital letter, as well as all sentences. A similar strong tendency is observable in earlier stages of English too, and although literary style is not absolutely consistent in this respect, there are many more capitals in the work of a poet like John Milton, for instance, than in written English today; see (2).

(2) Of Mans First Disobedience, and the Fruit
     Of that Forbidden Tree, whose mortal taste
     Brought Death into the World, and all our woe,
     With loss of *Eden*, till one greater Man
     Restore us, and regain the blissful Seat,
     Sing Heav'nly Muse …
          (Milton, *Paradise Lost*, Book 1, first 6 lines)

2.3 The phoneme

Children do not learn the rules of spoken language by explicit instruction, but rather by a combination of copying what they hear, and building up mental generalisations based on their experiences. How much they are helped in this by some internal structure in the brain dedicated to language acquisition, which linguists call a Language Acquisition Device or Language Faculty, is still a matter of debate.

Nonetheless, aspects of spoken language show very strong similarities to the types of patterns outlined above for writing. Again, some differences between units matter, because replacing one with another will cause a different meaning to be conveyed in the language in question: replace the initial sound [k] in *call* with [t], and you have *tall*, an entirely different English word. Correspondingly, English speakers perceive [k] and [t] as entirely separate sounds, and find them rather easy to distinguish.

In other cases, two sounds which phoneticians can equally easily tell apart will be regarded as the same by native speakers. For instance, say the phrase *kitchen cupboard* to yourself, and think about the first sounds of the two words. Despite the difference in spelling (another case where orthography, as we saw also in the last chapter, is not an entirely reliable guide to the sounds of a language), native speakers will tend to think of those initial consonants as the same – both are [k]s. However, if you say the phrase several times, slowly, and think uncharacteristically carefully about whether your articulators are doing the same at the beginning of both words, you will find that there is a discernible difference. For the first sound in *kitchen*, your tongue will be raised towards the roof of your mouth, further forward than for the beginning of *cupboard*; and for *kitchen*, your lips will be spread apart a little more too, while for *cupboard* your mouth will be more open. Unless you are from Australia or New Zealand (for reasons we shall discover in Chapter 8), this difference is even clearer from the phrase *car keys*, this time with the first word having the initial sound produced further back in the mouth, and the second further forward.

In IPA terms, these can be transcribed as [k], the *cupboard* sound, and [c], the *kitchen* one. However, in English [k] and [c] do not signal different meanings as [k] and [t] do in *call* versus *tall*; instead, we can always predict that [k] will appear before one set of vowels, which we call back vowels, like the [ʌ] of *cupboard* or the [ɑː] a Southern British English speaker has in *car*, while [c] appears before front vowels, like the [ɪ] of *kitchen* or the [iː] in Southern British English *keys*. Typically, speakers control predictable differences of this type automatically and subconsciously, and sometimes resist any suggestion that the sounds involved, like [k] and [c] in English, are different at all, requiring uncharacteristically close and persistent listening to tell the two apart. The difference between [k] and [c] in English is redundant; in phonological terms, this means the difference arises automatically in different contexts, but does not convey any new information.

Returning to our orthographic analogy, recall that every instance of a hand-written *a* or *A* will be different from every other instance, even produced by the same person. In just the same way, the same speaker producing the same words (say, multiple repetitions of *kitchen cupboard*) will produce minutely different instances of [k] and [c]. However, a hierarchical organisation of these variants can be made: in terms of spelling, we can characterise variants as belonging to the lower-case or capital set, and those in turn as realisations of the abstract grapheme <a>. The subclasses have a consistent and predictable distribution, with upper-case at the beginnings of proper nouns and sentences, and lower-case everywhere else: we can say that this distribution is rule-governed. Similarly again, we can classify all the variants we hear as belonging to either fronter [c] or backer [k], although we are not, at least without a little phonetic consciousness-raising, aware of that difference in the way we are with *a* and *A*; presumably the fact that we learn writing later, and with more explicit instruction, accounts for our higher level of awareness here.

In turn, [c] and [k], which native speakers regard as the same, are realisations of an abstract unit we call the phoneme (where the ending -*eme*, as in *grapheme*, means 'some abstract unit'). Phonemes appear between slash brackets, and are conventionally represented by IPA symbols, in this case /k/. As with graphemes, we could in principle use an abstract symbol for this abstract unit, say /§/, or /☺/, or give it a number or a name: but again, it is convenient and clear to use the same symbol as one of its realisations. Those realisations, here [k] and [c], are allophones of the phoneme /k/.

To qualify as allophones of the same phoneme, two (or more) phones, that is sounds, must meet two criteria. First, their distribution must be predictable: we must be able to specify where one will turn up, and where the other; and those sets of contexts must not overlap. If this is true, the two phones are said to be in complementary distribution. Second, if one phone is exceptionally substituted for the other in the same context, that substitution must not correspond to a meaning difference. Even if you say *kitchen cupboard* with the [k] first and the [c] second (and that won't be easy, because you have been doing the opposite as long as you have been speaking English – it will be even harder than trying to write at your normal speed while substituting small *a* for capital *A* and vice versa), another English speaker will only notice that there is something vaguely odd about your speech, if that. She may think you have an unfamiliar accent; but crucially, she will understand that you mean 'kitchen cupboard', and not something else. This would not be so where a realisation of one phoneme is replaced by a realisation of another: if the [k] allophone of /k/ is replaced by the [t] allophone of /t/, then *tall* will be understood instead of *call*.

Finally, just as the orthographic rules can vary between languages and across time, so no two languages or periods will have exactly the same phonology. Although in English [k] and [c] are allophones of the same phoneme, and are regarded as the same sound, in Hungarian they are different phonemes. We can test for this by looking for minimal pairs: that is, pairs of words differing in meaning, where the only difference in sound is that one has one of the two phones at issue where the other has the other (think of *tall* and *call*). In Hungarian, we find minimal pairs like *kuka* [kuka] 'dustbin' and *kutya* [kuca] 'dog'. It follows that [k] and [c] are not in complementary but in contrastive distribution; that inter-changing them does make a meaning difference between words; and hence that [k] and [c] belong to different phonemes, /k/ and /c/ respec-tively, in Hungarian. Unsurprisingly, speakers of Hungarian find the difference between [k] and [c] glaringly obvious, and would be extremely surprised to find that English speakers typically lump them together as the same sound.

As for differences between periods of the same language, it is straight-forward to demonstrate that Modern English [f] and [v] contrast, or are in complementary distribution, since minimal pairs like *fat* [f] versus *vat* [v], *leaf* versus *leave*, or *safer* versus *saver* are easy to come by. The phoneme system of Modern English therefore contains both /f/ and /v/. However, the situation was very different in Old English, as the examples in (3) show.

(3) *Old English*
    hla[v]ord <hlaford> 'lord'   hco[v]on <heofon> 'heaven'
    æ[f]ter <æfter> 'after'   [f]isc <fisc> 'fish'

    o[v]er <ofer> 'over'
    heal[f] <healf> 'half'

Instead of minimal pairs, we find predictable, complementary dis-tribution, with [v] appearing medially, between vowels, and [f] in other positions. Consequently, [f] and [v] can be analysed as allophones of one phoneme, which we might call /f/: Old English speakers would have regarded [f] and [v] as the same, just as Modern English speakers think of [k] and [c] as the same sound. Later in the history of English, many words like *very*, *virtue* and *veal* were borrowed from French, bringing with them initial [v], which had not previously been found in English. The distribution of [f] and [v] therefore ceased to be complementary, since both could appear in word-initial position, creating minimal pairs like *very* and *ferry*, or *veal* and *feel*. In consequence, [v] stopped being an allophone of /f/, and became a phoneme in its own right, producing the opposition of /f/ (realised as [f]) and /v/ (realised as [v]) we find today.

2.4 Some further examples

The notion of the phoneme is a notoriously difficult one to come to terms with at first. This is not altogether surprising: it isn't every day that you are told you know a whole range of things you didn't know you knew, and moreover that this knowledge seems likely to be structured in terms of a set of mental units you didn't know you had. However, the fact that phonemes are so central to phonology means it is well worth giving a few extra examples, to make the concept a little more familiar.

First, let us return to Modern English /t/ and /k/, which we have already met in *tall* versus *call*; in fact, we can add *Paul* to make a minimal triplet, adding /p/ to our phoneme system. Now hold a piece of paper up in front of your mouth by the bottom of the sheet, so the top is free to flap about, and try saying *Paul, tall, call*. You will find that a little puff of air is released after the initial /p/, /t/ and /k/, making the paper move slightly: this is called aspiration, and signalled in IPA transcription by adding a superscript [ʰ] after the symbol in question. This means that /p/, /t/ and /k/ have the allophones [pʰ], [tʰ] and [kʰ] word-initially; the aspiration is most noticeable with [pʰ], since it is articulated with the lips, nearest to where the air exits.

However, /p/, /t/ and /k/ really do have to be right at the beginning of the word for these allophones to appear. Try to make yourself aware of the initial aspiration in *pill, till* and *kill*; this time, you will again be producing [pʰ] and [tʰ], but the allophone of /k/ will be slightly different; the front vowel in *kill* conditions a fronter, aspirated [cʰ]. If you add an initial [s] and do the piece of paper trick again, you will find that there is no discernible movement. After [s], we find plain, unaspirated allophones [p], [t] and [c] in *spill, still* and *skill* (and unaspirated [k] in *scold*, as opposed to [kʰ] in *cold*, where /k/ is followed by a back vowel).

It follows that phonemes can have a whole range of allophones. Illustrating with just one phoneme, Modern English /k/, we have now identified word-initial aspirated [kʰ] in *call, cold*; fronter, aspirated [cʰ] before front vowels, as in *kill, kitchen*; unaspirated [k] in *scold*; and un-aspirated [c] in *skill*. That deals with the beginnings of words. At the ends, /k/ is very frequently accompanied by a partial glottal stop; this is known as glottal reinforcement, and the final sound in *back* is signalled in IPA terms as [ʔk]. When a following word begins with [g], for instance, this [ʔk] is sometimes replaced by a glottal stop, as in *back garden*, where you may perceive the [ʔ] allophone of /k/ as almost a pause before the [g]. Glottalisation of this kind is much more common for /t/: as we saw in the last chapter, glottal stops are increasingly found in non-standard accents in forms like *statement, seatbelt, butter*, meaning that the glottal stop in English can be an allophone of both /k/ and /t/. We return to this issue of overlap in Chapter 5.

For a final example, let us turn to a phoneme we have not considered before, namely /l/. /l/ has only two main allophones in English, depending on its position in the word (unless you speak some varieties of Irish or Welsh English, or Geordie, the variety spoken around Newcastle, in which case you have only the first realisation described below; conversely, some varieties of Scottish English only have the second allophone). If you say *lull*, or *lilt*, you will notice that the first *l* in each case is pronounced with the tip of your tongue up behind your top front teeth, while the second additionally has the tongue raised further back. This time the distribution of the allophones does not depend on the frontness or backness of the adjacent vowel, since *lull* has a back vowel, while *lilt* has a front one, but both have the fronter [l] first, and the backer [ɫ] second. In the case of /l/, what matters (roughly speaking; we will come up with a better generalisation in Chapter 9) is whether the /l/ precedes or follows the vowel in the word. If /l/ comes first, it is pronounced as 'clear', fronter [l], as also in *clear*; and if the vowel comes first, /l/ is realised as 'dark', more back [ɫ], as in *dull*. The two are obviously in complementary distribution, and hence can both straightforwardly be assigned to the same phoneme, /l/, in Modern English.

We find a different story in Scots Gaelic, however, where minimal pairs can be found for the clear and dark variants. For instance, the words *baile* 'a town' and *balla* 'a wall' are pronounced identically, except for the clear [l] in *baile*, and the dark [ɫ] in *balla*. Whereas substituting clear for dark pronunciations, or vice versa, in English would be picked up by listeners as slightly, intangibly peculiar, for a Scots Gaelic speaker the difference is both easily noticeable and meaningful, since a substitution will simply produce the wrong word. Again, we find that differences which in one language are automatic to the point of inaudibility without training, are highly salient and have important linguistic consequences in another.

2.5 The reality of the phoneme

We have already seen that the phoneme system of a speaker's native language, and specifically the difference between pairs of sounds which contrast and pairs which do not, strongly condition her perceptions: the early twentieth century American linguist Sapir concludes that 'What the native speaker hears is not phonetic elements but phonemes'. However, the phoneme is a psychologically real unit in other ways too, since it does not only condition what we hear, but also what we do.

First, alphabetic spelling systems are frequently based on the phonemes of a language: there are various reported cases of linguists teaching variants of the IPA to speakers of languages which lacked orthographies, and providing inventories of symbols which covered all the phones of the language, but where speakers subsequently made use of only one symbol per phoneme. In Old English, both [f] and [v], which were then in complementary distribution, were spelled <f>, whereas in Modern English contrastive /f/ and /v/ typically correspond to <f> (or <ph>) versus <v>. Similarly, in Hungarian /k/ and /c/ are consistently distinguished as <k> and <ty>. The alphabet has several times been borrowed by speakers of one language from those of another, and has been remodelled in some respects to fit the borrowing phoneme system better. So, the first letter of the Semitic alphabet represents the glottal stop, [ʔ], which is phonemically distinctive in Arabic, for example: but when this alphabet was borrowed by the Greeks, that first letter, Greek alpha, was taken to represent the vowel which begins the word *alpha* itself. Although Greek speakers would commonly produce an initial glottal stop on a word like *alpha* (as would English speakers, especially when saying the word emphatically), they would not observe it or want to symbolise it, since [ʔ] is not a phoneme of Greek. We should not, however, as we saw in the last chapter, assume that we can simply read the phoneme system off the spelling system, since there is not always a one-to-one correlation. Hence, English does have two orthographic symbols for /k/, namely <k> and <c>, but these do not systematically signal two separate allophones: the spelling system simply has a redundant extra symbol here. Furthermore, some phonemes are spelled consistently, but not with a single graph, so the phonemic difference between the English nasals /m/, /n/ and /ŋ/ in *ram, ran* and *rang*, is signalled orthographically by <m>, <n> and <ng> (or <nk> in *rank*).

More importantly, our native phoneme system tends to get in the way when we try to learn other languages. It is perhaps unsurprising that we should find it difficult at first to produce sounds which do not figure at all in our first language. However, it is just as difficult, and sometimes worse, to learn sounds which are phonemically contrastive in the language we are learning, but allophones of a single phoneme in our native system. For instance, there is no contrast between aspirated [tʰ] and unaspirated [t] in English; we can predict that the former appears only word-initially. In Chengtu Chinese, however, /t/ contrasts with /tʰ/, as we find minimal pairs like [tou] 'a unit of dry measure for grain' versus [tʰou] 'to tremble'; the same is true in Thai, where [tam] 'to pound' contrasts with [tʰam] 'to do', establishing a phonemic distinction of /t/ and /tʰ/. When a native English speaker tries to learn Chengtu Chinese, or Thai, she will find this distinction extremely awkward to replicate, despite the fact that she herself has always used both these sounds. The problem is that, whereas a totally new and unfamiliar sound simply has to be learned from scratch, an old sound in a new role requires further processes of adjustment: our English speaking Thai learner has to suppress her instinctive and subconscious division of the aspirated and unaspirated sounds, and learn to produce both in the same context. In perceptual terms, it is again easier to hear a completely new sound, which will initially be extremely easy to perceive because of its very unfamiliarity, than to learn to distinguish two sounds which have conceptually been considered as one and the same. Conversely, a Korean speaker, who has [r] and [l] as allophones of a single phoneme, with [r] produced between vowels and [l] everywhere else, will make errors in learning English, finding minimal pairs like *lot* and *rot* highly counter-intuitive, and tending to produce [l] at the beginning of both, but [r] medially in both *lolly* and *lorry*. A combination of unlearning and learning are needed to get those patterns right.

In Chapter 4, we shall return to phonemes and allophones, and develop more precise ways of stating exactly where each allophone occurs. First, however, we need some more phonetic detail on the consonants of English, and some more technical vocabulary to describe how they are produced.

Exercises

1. A learner of English as a second language has the following pronunciations (note that [ʃ] is the symbol for the first sound in *ship*, and [ð] for the first sound in *the*):

that [dat]	*dog* [dɒg]	*head* [hɛd]
leather [lɛðə]	*leader* [liːðə]	
sing [ʃɪŋ]	*sat* [sat]	*loss* [lɒs]
fish [fɪʃ]	*miss* [mɪʃ]	*push* [pus]

How might you explain these non-native pronunciations? How do you think this learner would pronounce the bold-faced consonants in ***D**add**y***, *ei**th**er*, *loa**th**e*; ***s**hip*, *pa**ss**, di**sh**, u**sh**er*?

2. Do the following sounds contrast in English? Find minimal pairs to support your hypothesis, ideally for initial, medial and final position in the word. Where minimal pairs for all positions do not seem to be available, write a short statement of where the sound in question can and cannot be found.

[m n ŋ p b t d k g l r]

3. The Ministry for Education in a certain country whose language has up to now been unwritten has hired two foreign linguists to produce an orthography. Linguists A and B have suggested two rather different systems. Which one is most in line with the phonological structure of the

language it is designed for? Why do you think the other linguist may have made different decisions?

Linguist A	Linguist B	pronunciation	meaning
bim	bim	[bim]	'rug'
bin	bin	[bin]	'head'
biŋ	bing	[biŋ]	'wheel'
zag	zak	[zak]	'parrot'
zib	zip	[zip]	'ostrich'
azaŋ	azang	[azaŋ]	'to speak'
obaz	obas	[obas]	'to throw'
ham	ham	[ham]	'egg'
mohiz	mohis	[mohis]	'to eat'
zigah	ziga	[zigah]	'to sing'
gig	gik	[gik]	'ant'
gah	ga	[gah]	'a song'
nagog	nagok	[nagok]	'to sting'
habiz	habis	[habis]	'to drink'

Recommendations for reading

Further discussion of phoneme analysis can be found in a number of recent textbooks on English phonology or phonology in general. Carr (1999), and Davenport and Hannahs (1998), provide brief, approachable outlines; Giegerich (1992) is written at a slightly higher level, and also deals with more theoretical shortcomings of the phoneme. Students interested in writing systems, and in the history of writing, might consult Sampson (1985) or Coulmas (1988). Issues of language acquisition and the question of innateness are debated in Pinker (1994).

3 Describing English consonants

3.1 What's inside a phonetic symbol?

So far, we have considered the IPA essentially as an alternative writing system, which allows us to express a larger range of sounds than the English spelling system would. However, looking only at those symbols might suggest that we are dealing with individual, self-contained units when we consider phonemes and allophones: each is like a locked black box labelled with an IPA symbol.

In fact, each IPA symbol is shorthand for a whole range of properties, and those properties explain how the particular segment being symbolised is pronounced; unpacking the black box for each sound reveals not a jumble, but an internal structure, and understanding that structure allows us to make comparisons with other sounds. When we know that [k], for instance, is a voiceless velar plosive, we can start to see what properties it shares with other sounds which might also be voiceless, or velar, or plosives; we can also see how it differs from other sounds which are not voiceless, or velar, or plosives. Furthermore, we shall see what properties different allophones of the same phoneme share, which might allow them to be regarded as 'the same' by speakers of English: that is, we can work out what particular phonetic features speakers of English tend to ignore, and which they are aware of. Since this may be very different for speakers of other languages, unpacking IPA notation in this way also allows cross-linguistic comparisons to be made. In this chapter, we shall therefore consider a very basic set of phonetic features which enable us to describe the articulation of the consonants of English, and to assess their differences and similarities.

3.2 Consonant classification

A biologist looking at some particular creature wants to know various things about it, to work out where it should be placed in conventional biological classification. Some properties are visible and therefore easy to work out, such as how many legs it has or whether it has fur, feathers or scales. In other cases, closer observation will be needed: tooth shape cannot usually be checked from a distance. Still other properties are behavioural, and our biologist might need to observe her creature over a longer period of time to figure out whether it lays eggs or bears live young, or what it eats.

The same goes for phonetic classification: some properties are straight-forwardly observable when you look in a mirror, or can be figured out easily from feeling what your articulators are doing. Other features are harder to spot, and need some extra training before you will become aware of them. Furthermore, we also need to remember that phonemes are realised as various different allophones, so we must build up a picture of all the possible environments where that phoneme can occur and what happens there, to sort out how it behaves.

Biologists today are, of course, working within an agreed classifi-cation: when they observe a creature with particular physical traits, or particular behaviours, they can slot it into a framework of herbivores and carnivores; mammals, insects, birds and reptiles; vertebrates and invert-ebrates; and so on. Fortunately, phoneticians and phonologists have a similar, generally agreed framework for sounds. For consonants, we need to know six things to arrive at a classification: in the rest of this chapter, we shall consider these six sets of properties in turn, and assess which English phonemes fit into each category. Vowel classification involves rather different features, and we return to this in Chapter 6: we are beginning with consonants because many of their properties are easier to ascertain from self-observation, and because the systems of consonant phonemes in different accents of English vary far less than the vowels.

3.3 The anatomy of a consonant

3.3.1 What is the airstream mechanism?

Speech is audible because the movements of articulators (to be discussed in subsequent sections) cause the air to vibrate, forming sound waves which travel to the hearer's ears, and set up vibrations in her inner ear, which are then translated into sounds again by the brain. Since sound waves need air, it follows that articulatory vibrations will only make sound waves if there is a moving body of air available. Airstreams can be set in motion, or initiated, in three ways; however, only one is used in English, and indeed is found in every language of the world.

Essentially, speaking is modified breathing: it makes use of the resources involved in normal respiration, but in a more controlled way. When we are simply breathing quietly, the phases of breathing in and out last approximately the same time, and expiration is not under our physical control; it simply occurs as an automatic consequence of having breathed in. However, when we are speaking, the phase of breathing out is significantly longer, depending on the length of the utterance we want to produce. A network of muscles, like the intercostal muscles between our ribs, come into play to make breathing out smoother, more gradual and more controlled during speech, providing a regular flow of air which can then be modified by the articulators in various ways.

All the sounds of English, both consonants and vowels, are produced on this pulmonic egressive airstream, where the initiator is the lungs and the rest of the respiratory system, and the direction of airflow is outwards: this is overwhelmingly the most common airstream mechanism in every language of the world. It can generally be taken for granted that the sounds under discussion below are pulmonic egressive, but you should remember to give that information in a complete description: so the labial nasal [m] (which, as we shall see, is produced using the lips – hence labial, and with airflow through the nose – hence nasal), is strictly a pulmonic egressive labial nasal.

It is possible to produce speech using a pulmonic ingressive airstream. No language seems to use this airstream regularly for particular sounds, although it has been reported in various cultures as a means of voice disguise: if you try to breathe in and speak at the same time, you will find that the pitch of your voice raises significantly.

There are two other airstreams which may be involved in speech, although even in languages where these are used, they will characterise only a few sounds, interpolated in a stream of pulmonic egressive speech. The first is the glottalic airstream mechanism, initiated by a movement of the larynx, which is where you can feel your 'Adam's apple' protruding slightly about half-way up your throat. The larynx can move up or down, and the glottalic airstream can therefore be either ingressive or egressive, producing sounds known as implosives and ejectives respectively; none of these occur in English. Finally, the 'tut-tut' click sound [|] is produced on a velaric airstream, which operates only ingressively. When you make [|] you can feel that the back of your tongue is pressed against the roof of your mouth, stopping air from moving any further back; a little air is then drawn into the mouth further forward, and the closure with the tongue is released to make a click. Neither the glottalic nor the velaric airstreams provide airflow with the volume or controllability of the pulmonic system.

3.3.2 Voiced or voiceless?

A major division among speech sounds which is relevant for all languages is the dichotomy of voiced and voiceless. If you put your fingers on your 'Adam's apple' or 'voicebox' (technically the larynx), and produce a very long [zzzzzzz], you should feel vibration; this shows that [z] is a voiced sound. On the other hand, if you make a very long [sssssss], you will not feel the same sort of activity: [s] is a voiceless sound.

Pulmonic egressive air flows through the trachea, or windpipe, and up into the larynx, which is like a mobile little box suspended at the top of the trachea, acting to control the airway to and from the lungs, with the epiglottis above it protecting the lungs by stopping foreign bodies like food from dropping in. Stretched across the larynx from front to back are the vocal folds, or vocal cords. These can be pulled back and drawn apart, in which case they leave a free space, the glottis, through which air can flow: this is the case for voiceless sounds like [s]. For voiced sounds, the vocal folds are drawn together, closing off the glottis; however, the pressure of air flowing from the lungs will cause the folds to part, and their essentially elastic nature will then force them together again. Repetitions of this cycle of opening and closing cause vibration, as for [z]. The number of cycles of opening and closing per second will depend on the size of the vocal folds, and determines the pitch of the voice: hence, children's smaller, shorter vocal folds produce their higher voices. Although sounds can be voiced in any position in the word, voicing is most obvious medially, between other voiced sounds: when there is an adjacent voiceless sound or pause, voicing will not last for so long or be so strong. Consequently, although English has the minimal pairs *tip – dip*, *latter – ladder*, *bit – bid* for /t/ versus /d/, [d] is only voiced throughout its production in *ladder*, where it is medial and surrounded by voiced vowels. Word-initially, we are more likely to identify /t/ in *tip* by its aspiration, and /d/ in *dip* by lack of aspiration, than rely on voicing.

Voicelessness and voicing are the two main settings of phonation, or states of the glottis: for English at least, the only other relevant case, and again one which is used paralinguistically, is whisper. In whisper phonation, the vocal folds are close together but not closed; the reduced size of the glottis allows air to pass, but with some turbulence which is heard as the characteristic hiss of whisper.

3.3.3 Oral or nasal?

The next major issue is where the pulmonic egressive airstream used in English goes. For most sounds, air passes from the lungs, up through a

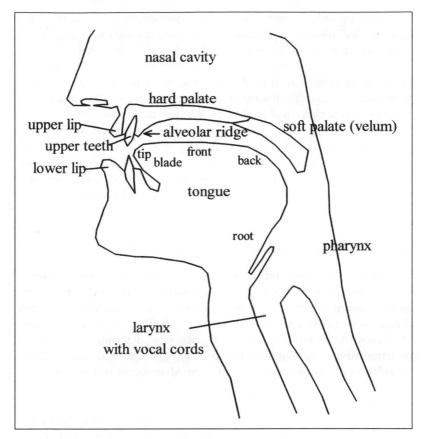

Figure 3.1 The vocal tract

long tube composed of the trachea, or windpipe; the larynx; and the pharynx, which opens out into the back of the oral cavity. The air passes the various articulators in the mouth, and exits at the lips; and all these vocal organs are shown in Figure 3.1. However, for three English sounds, air passes through the nasal cavity instead.

The key to whether air can flow through the nose is the velum, or soft palate, which you can identify by curling the tip of your tongue up and running it back along the roof of your mouth until you feel the hard, bony palate giving way to something squashier. For oral sounds, the velum is raised and pushed against the back wall of the pharynx, cutting off access to the nose. However, for [m], [n] and [ŋ] in *ram*, *ran* and *rang*, the velum is lowered, so that air moving up from the lungs must flow through the nose. If you produce a long [s], you will be able to feel that air is passing only through your mouth; conversely, if you hum a long [m], you will notice that air continues to flow through your nose while your lips are pressed together, with that closure being released only at the end of the [m]. When someone suffering from a cold tells you 'I've got a cold id by dose' instead of 'I've got a cold in my nose', she is failing to produce [n] and [m] because soft tissue swelling blocks air access to the nose and perforce makes all sounds temporarily oral.

Nasal sounds, like [m] and [n], are produced with air only passing through the nasal cavity for at least part of their production. On the other hand, nasalised sounds, like the vowel in *can*, preceding a nasal consonant, as opposed to the vowel in *cat*, which precedes an oral one, are characterised by airflow through both nose and mouth simultaneously.

3.3.4 What is the manner of articulation?

To produce any consonant, an active articulator, usually located somewhere along the base of the vocal tract, moves towards a passive articulator, somewhere along the top. Where those articulators are, determines the consonant's place of articulation, as we shall see in the next section. How close the active and passive articulators get, determines the manner of articulation. There are three main manners of articulation, and one subsidiary case which in a sense is intermediate between the first two.

A. STOPS

If the active and passive articulators actually touch, stopping airflow through the oral cavity completely for a brief period, the sound articulated is a stop. If you put your lips together to produce [p] *pea*, and hold them in that position, you will feel the build-up of air which is then released when you move from the stop to the following vowel. Further back in the vocal tract, [t] *tea* and [k] *key* are also stop sounds. More accurately, all these are plosives, the term for oral stops produced on a pulmonic egressive airstream, just as clicks are stops produced on a velaric ingressive airstream, for instance. Plosives may be voiceless, like [p], [t] and [k], or voiced, like their equivalents [b], [d] and [g].

Since the definition of a stop involves the complete, transient obstruction of the *oral* cavity, it also includes nasal sounds, where airflow continues through the nose. English [m], [n] and [ŋ] are therefore nasal stops, although they are typically referred to simply as nasals, as there are no distinctive English nasals involving other manners of articulation. All these nasals are also voiced.

Finally, some varieties of English also have subtypes of stops known as taps or trills. While a plosive is characterised by a complete obstruction of oral airflow, followed generally by release of that airflow, a tap is a very quick, ballistic movement where the active articulator strikes a glancing blow against the passive one; interruption of the airstream is real, but extremely brief. Many Scots speakers have a tapped allophone [ɾ] of the phoneme /r/ between vowels, as in *arrow, very*; many American speakers have a similar tap as a realisation of /t/ in *butter, water*. Trills are repeated taps, where the active articulator vibrates against the passive one. Trilled [r] is now rather uncommon for speakers of English, although attempts at imitating Scots often involve furious rolling of [r]s.

B. FRICATIVES

During the production of a fricative, the active and passive articulators are brought close together, but not near enough to totally block the oral cavity. This close approximation of the articulators means the air coming from the lungs has to squeeze through a narrow gap at high speed, creating turbulence, or local audible friction, which is heard as hissing for a voiceless fricative, and buzzing for a voiced one. English [f] *five* and [s] *size* are voiceless fricatives, while [v] *five* and [z] *size* are voiced.

The subclass of affricates consists of sounds which start as stops and end up as fricatives; but as we shall see in Chapter 5, they behave as single, complex sounds rather than sequences. Stops generally involve quick release of their complete articulatory closure; but if this release is slow, or delayed, the articulators will pass through a stage of close approximation appropriate for a fricative. The two relevant sounds for English are [tʃ], at the beginning and end of *church*, and its voiced equivalent [dʒ], found at the beginning and end of *judge*. If you pronounce these words extremely slowly, you should be able to identify the stop and fricative phases.

C. APPROXIMANTS

It is relatively easy to recognise a stop or fricative, and to diagnose the articulators involved, since these are either touching or so close that their location can be felt. In approximants, on the other hand, the active and passive articulator never become sufficiently close to create audible friction. Instead, the open approximation of the articulators alters the shape of the oral cavity, and leads to the production of a particular sound quality.

There are four approximant consonant phonemes in English: /j/ *yes*, /w/ *wet*, /r/ *red* (although as we have seen, /r/ may have a tapped allophone for some speakers) and /l/ *let*. All these approximants are voiced.

3.3.5 Is the airflow central or lateral?

This parameter is rather a minor one, since it distinguishes only one phoneme of English from all others. For almost all English consonants, the airflow through the oral cavity is central. Recall that fricatives, like [s] or [f], are produced with close approximation of the active and passive articulators; however, if you produce any fricative, you will feel that your articulators are actually pushed together quite tightly at the sides of the oral cavity, with the actual close approximation, and hence the narrow gap for airflow, left in the middle. The same is true for all the approximants except one: if you produce *rip* and *lip*, and focus on the initial consonants, you will notice that while the outgoing air for /r/, as usual, moves along the centre of the mouth, for /l/ it moves down the sides. If you find this difficult to feel, try making the related voiceless fricative sound found in Welsh names spelled with <ll>, like *Llewellyn*; because this is a fricative and involves close approximation of the articulators, the airflow is easier to observe. Alternatively, try making an [l] ingressively, pulling the air into your mouth instead of breathing it out, and feel the cold air moving inwards along the sides of your tongue. In English, both the clear and the dark allophones of /l/, and only these, have lateral airflow, and are known as lateral approximants.

Since the only case where the central versus lateral difference is distinctive in English involves /r/ and /l/, these should consistently be described as central and lateral respectively. Although in a particularly thorough description, all other sounds (except nasals, which have no oral airflow at all) should be explicitly stated to be central, this definition will generally be understood rather than stated below, since the other English sounds do not contrast with lateral sounds of the same place and manner of articulation, meaning that confusion is highly unlikely.

3.3.6 What is the place of articulation?

As we have seen, the location of the active and passive articulators determines the place of articulation for a consonant. In English, consonants are produced at eight places of articulation. Since we have now covered all the other articulatory parameters required to describe consonants, introducing and defining these places will allow us to build up a complete consonant phoneme system for English. In the tables below, the phoneme or allophone in question is initial in the example word, unless another part of that word is bold-face.

A. BILABIAL

For a bilabial sound, the active articulator is the bottom lip, and the passive articulator is the top lip.

/p/	*pie*	voiceless bilabial plosive
/b/	*by*	voiced bilabial plosive
/m/	*my*	voiced bilabial nasal

There is at least one further English phoneme which to an extent fits under this heading: this is the approximant /w/ in *wet*. In producing [w], the lips are certainly approximated, though not enough to cause friction or obstruct the airflow; but you should be able to feel that the back of your tongue is also bunched up. This additional articulation takes place at the velum, so that [w] is not simply a labial sound, but a labial-velar one. In some accents of English, notably those spoken in Scotland and New Zealand, this /w/ contrasts with /ʍ/, the voiceless labial-velar fricative, which tends to occur in words spelled <wh->. If you have the same pronunciation for *witch* and *which*, or *Wales* and *whales*, then you have only /w/; if these are consistently different for you, then these minimal pairs establish a contrast of /w/ and /ʍ/.

/w/	*witch*	voiced labial-velar approximant
/ʍ/	*which*	voiceless labial-velar fricative

B. LABIO-DENTAL

For labio-dental sounds, the active articulator is again the bottom lip, but this time it moves up to the top front teeth. Note that these sounds are labio-dental, while /w/ and /ʍ/ are labial-velar, because in the first case, articulation takes place only at a single location, while in the second, there are two separate, simultaneous articulations.

/f/	*fat*	voiceless labio-dental fricative
/v/	*vat*	voiced labio-dental fricative

C. DENTAL

In most English sounds, and most speech sounds in general, the active articulator is part of the tongue; to avoid confusion, places of articulation where the tongue is involved are therefore generally called after the passive articulator. For the two dental fricatives, it follows that the passive articulator is the top front teeth; the active articulator is the tip of the tongue. The tongue itself is conventionally divided into the tip (the very front); the blade (just behind the blade, and lying opposite the alveolar ridge); the front (just behind the blade, and lying opposite the hard palate); the back (behind the front, and lying opposite the velum); and the root (right at the base, lying opposite the wall of the pharynx).

| [θ] | *thigh* | voiceless dental fricative |
| [ð] | *thy* | voiced dental fricative |

D. ALVEOLAR

Alveolar sounds are produced by the tip or blade of the tongue moving up towards the alveolar ridge, the bony protrusion you can feel if you curl your tongue back just behind your top front teeth.

/t/	*tie*	voiceless alveolar plosive
/d/	*die*	voiced alveolar plosive
/n/	*nigh*	voiced alveolar nasal
/s/	*sip*	voiceless alveolar fricative
/z/	*zip*	voiced alveolar fricative
/r/	*rip*	voiced alveolar central approximant
/l/	*lip*	voiced alveolar lateral approximant

The symbol /r/ is used for the phoneme here and throughout the book, primarily because it is typographically convenient; but different realisations of /r/ are found throughout the English-speaking world, and as we have seen, [r] itself, the voiced alveolar trill, is rather rare. The tapped realisation, [ɾ], is also alveolar; but another even more common pronunciation is not. This is the voiced retroflex approximant, [ɹ], which is produced with the tip of the tongue curled back slightly behind the alveolar ridge; this is the most common realisation of /r/ for speakers of Southern Standard British English and General American.

E. POSTALVEOLAR

If you move your tongue tip back behind the alveolar ridge, you will feel the hard palate, which then, moving further back again, becomes the soft palate, or velum. Postalveolar sounds are produced with the blade of the tongue as the active articulator, and the adjoining parts of the alveolar ridge and the hard palate as the passive one. They include two fricatives, and the affricates introduced in the last section.

/ʃ/	*ship*	voiceless postalveolar fricative
/ʒ/	*beige*	voiced postalveolar fricative
/tʃ/	*chunk*	voiceless postalveolar affricate
/dʒ/	*junk*	voiced postalveolar affricate

F. PALATAL

Palatals are produced by the front of the tongue, which moves up towards the hard palate. We have so far encountered two palatal sounds: the approximant /j/ in *yes*, and the voiceless palatal stop [c] in *kitchen*. Recall, however, that [c] is the allophone of /k/ found before certain vowels; velar [k] appears elsewhere. There is a similar pattern for /g/, which has as allophones velar [g] in *garden* and palatal [ɟ] *give*. Since we are constructing a phoneme system here, these allophones are not included in the list.

/j/	*yes*	voiced palatal approximant

G. VELAR

For velar sounds, the active articulator is the back of the tongue, and the passive articulator is the velum, or soft palate. The labial-velar approximant and fricative /w/ and /ʍ/ are not included here, as they were discussed above with the bilabials; however, it should be remembered that these doubly-articulated sounds strictly belong under both headings. Similarly, although the 'dark l' realisation, [ɫ], is also velar, it does not appear in the list below as it is an allophone of /l/.

There is a further accent difference involving velar sounds: in some varieties of English, notably Scottish ones, there is a voiceless velar fricative, /x/: this is the sound at the end of Scots *loch*, which speakers of other accents typically replace with a [k].

/k/	*cot*	voiceless velar plosive
/g/	*got*	voiced velar plosive
/ŋ/	*rang*	voiced velar nasal
/x/	*loch*	voiceless velar fricative

H. GLOTTAL

Glottal sounds are in the minority in articulatory terms, since they do not involve the tongue: instead, the articulators are the vocal folds, which constitute a place of articulation as well as having a crucial role in voicing. English has two glottal sounds. The first is allophonic, namely the glottal stop, [ʔ], which appears as an intervocalic realisation of /t/ in many accents, as in *butter*. The glottal stop is technically voiceless, though in fact it could hardly be anything else, since when the vocal folds are pressed together to completely obstruct the airstream, as must be the case for a stop sound, air cannot simultaneously be passing through to cause vibration. The second, the voiceless glottal fricative [h], is a phoneme in its own right.

/h/	*high*	voiceless glottal fricative

Exercises

1. (a) Which of the following words begin with a voiceless fricative?

    hang   dogs   cut   ship   chip   foot   zip   sit

   (b) Which of the following words begin with a voiced sound?

    nap   jug   knock lot   pet   jump   fin

   (c) Which of the following words ends with a stop sound?

    nap   hang   jug   nudge bet   lamb   lots

   (d) Which of the following words ends with an alveolar sound?

    pot   sad   boss   lamb   lamp   size   hen   call

   (e) Which of the following words contain an approximant consonant?

    wash   hall   map   sing   sigh   red   yellow

2. (a) What do the initial consonants of these words have in common?

    wash   let   right   yet   wish   rough

   (b) What do the final consonants of these words have in common?

    hop   hot   pass   wish   rough lock   scratch

   (c) What do the initial consonants of these words have in common?

    fish   ship   zip   sigh   house   view

3. How do the consonants at the end of the words in List A differ from those at the end of the words in List B?

	List A	List B
(a)	ham	top
	sin	lock
	sing	rot

    If you say [sɪŋg], ignore the final [g] for this exercise.

	List A	List B
(b)	place	lake
	lose	beg
	half	dot
(c)	dogs	rough
	hall	cats
	film	catch
	cold	help

4. Transcribe the words below. Then write as full a description as you can of all the consonants in each word, in your accent. For instance, in *doze* [d] is a pulmonic egressive central voiced alveolar stop; [z] is a pulmonic egressive central voiced alveolar fricative. Remember to pay attention to the sounds, and not to the spelling.

  psalm jester which climb heavy splint loch bought squelch

Recommendations for reading

Of the textbooks recommended in the last chapter, Davenport and Hannahs (1998) provides the most accessible and comprehensive introduction to articulatory phonetics, as well as a useful chapter on acoustic phonetics, which is not dealt with here. Some useful general introductions to phonetics are Roach (2001), which may be of special help to non-native speakers; Ball and Rahilly (1999); Catford (1988); and Ladefoged (1983). The most comprehensive account of our current understanding of phonetics is Laver (1994). References relating particularly to the IPA were given in Chapter 1.

4 Defining distributions: consonant allophones

4.1 Phonemes revisited

As we saw in Chapter 3, the two major criteria for establishing phonemic contrast are predictability of occurrence, and invariance of meaning. That is to say, if we are dealing with two allophones of the same phoneme, the two must occur in non-overlapping sets of environments. Furthermore, there cannot be any minimal pairs, where substituting one of our focus sounds for the other in exactly the same context creates a difference in meaning. These two criteria establish conclusively that English [ɹ] and [l] belong to distinct phonemes: there are many minimal pairs, like *rip* and *lip*, *rot* and *lot*, *marrow* and *mallow*, so clearly the two phones occur in the same contexts; and substituting one for the other does create a meaning difference. On the other hand, clear, alveolar [l] and dark, velar [ɫ] occur in predictably different environments: in Standard Southern British English, the clear, more front one appears word-initially or between vowels, as in *lip*, *lot*, *mallow*, and the dark, more back one word-finally or before a consonant, as in *pill*, *tall*, *halt*. Since there are no minimal pairs, and substituting one variant for the other will not make a meaning difference, [l] and [ɫ] are necessarily allophones of a single phoneme, /l/.

Equipped with the articulatory descriptions from the last chapter, we can now progress to a more detailed account of the distribution of allophones. In doing so, we will also discover that certain phonemes form groups, in that they have similar allophones in similar environments. We must try to identify what members of such groups have in common, and what makes certain phonemes work together.

4.2 Making generalisations

In Chapter 2, several examples of allophonic variation were considered. In one case, we found that /k/ has two variant pronunciations, namely velar [k] in *cupboard* and palatal [c] in *kitchen*. Another involved /p/, /t/ and /k/, which have aspirated allophones, with a perceptible release of air, in *pill*, *till* and *kill*, but unaspirated allophones in *spill*, *still* and *skill*, or *sip*, *sit* and *sick*.

However, providing a list of words where the relevant allophone appears is only our starting point. Phonologists are interested in generalisations about the language they are working on, and indeed in generalisations about language in general; and generalisations are not best expressed simply as lists, as these do not reveal the factors which the forms in the lists have in common. Identifying these factors will help us to understand why the particular allophone appears in that context and not elsewhere, and to predict what will happen in other words with a similar context.

As an example, recall the [c] and [k] allophones of /k/. English speakers (with the exception of New Zealanders and Australians) will have palatal and velar pronunciations distributed as in (1).

(1) kitchen   [cɪtʃən]   keys   [ciːz]
     cupboard   [kʌbəd]   car   [kɑː]

If you were asked to predict the pronunciation of the initial sounds of *keep*, *cool*, *ceilidh* (for non-Scots, pronounced exactly as *Kayleigh*) and *koala*, you would not get very far by considering (1) as just two lists of words: how could you tell whether each of these examples fitted into the [c] list or the [k] list? The key is to consider what connects the words where each allophone appears: and the answer is that [c] appears before a front vowel (more detail on vowels is in Chapter 6), while [k] precedes a back vowel. It follows that *keep* and *ceilidh* will also have [c], since the bold-faced vowels are front, while *cool* and *koala* will have [k], as the bold-faced vowels are back. Since front vowels are made roughly at the hard palate, and so is palatal [c], while back vowels are produced at the velum, as is velar [k], the pairs of vowels and consonants 'match'. It is extremely common for sounds to become more similar, or to assimilate to one another, in this sort of way. As the previous chapter showed, the vocal organs undergo very complex, coordinated movements during speech, and anything that simplifies the gymnastics involved while not jeopardising comprehension is understandably very welcome to speakers. Specifying what the different examples have in common therefore allows us to understand the results we find, and make predictions about the behaviour of other forms with the same environment. And as we might expect, /g/, which matches /k/ in every respect except voicing, behaves in exactly the same way, being palatalised before the same set of vowels as /k/ in the same varieties.

In the case of /p/, /t/ and /k/ aspiration, the relevant conditioning factor is not the shape of an adjacent segment, but rather position in the word (more accurately, as we shall see in Chapter 9, in the syllable). What *pill, till* and *kill* have in common (along with *peel, pass, play, pretty* and many others) is that the /p/, /t/ or /k/ is right at the beginning of the word. In *spill, still, skill, sip, sit* and *sick,* and many others, it is not right at the beginning of the word; either another consonant precedes it, or it is word-final. We can test this hypothesis by finding lots of other examples where /p/, /t/ and /k/ appear word-initially, and checking whether there is aspiration. So long as we keep finding aspirated allophones there, and nowhere else, our generalisation holds. If we find counterexamples, where either aspirated forms appear in other contexts, or word-initial allophones of /p/, /t/ or /k/ are not aspirated, we have to modify our generalisation to include them. After a while, when we keep finding data that agree with our observation and not finding data that disagree, we can feel more confident that our generalisation is the right one, and regard our hypothesis as confirmed.

4.3 Making statements more precise

The next question is how we should express these generalisations. Having established that certain sounds are allophones of the same phoneme, and that they are in complementary distribution, we might write a statement like (2) to say what happens to the phoneme or phonemes in question, and where.

(2) a. /k/ and /g/ become [c] and [ɟ] when they are followed by a front vowel. They are pronounced as [k] and [g] in all other contexts.
   b. /p/, /t/ and /k/ become [pʰ], [tʰ] and [kʰ] at the very beginning of a word. In other contexts (i.e. after another consonant or at the end of a word), they are pronounced as [p], [t] and [k].

These statements express the main generalisation in each case. However, making a statement in normal English can be unclear and unwieldy, so phonologists typically use a more formal notation which helps us to work out exactly what is being said; it is easier that way to identify what a counterexample would be, and to see what predictions are being made. The English statement also does not tell us why /p/, /t/ and /k/ are affected, rather than just one or two of them; or why these three sounds should behave similarly, rather than /p/, /s/ and /r/, for instance. Similarly, we cannot see what /k/ and /g/ have in common, or indeed what the resulting allophones have in common, simply by looking at the phoneme symbols.

Introducing the articulatory descriptions from Chapter 3 immediately makes our statements more adequate and more precise, as we can now express what particular sets of sounds have in common (3).

(3) a. Velar stops become palatal when they are followed by a front vowel. They are pronounced as velar in all other contexts.

    b. Voiceless stops are aspirated at the very beginning of a word. Elsewhere, they are unaspirated.

We can take this one step further by regarding each of the articulatory descriptions as a binary feature: that is, a sound is either voiceless or voiced, and these are opposites; similarly, a sound is either nasal or not nasal. Instead of voiced and voiceless, or oral and nasal, we can then write [+voice] and [−voice], and [−nasal] and [+nasal]. This may seem like introducing needless complexity; but once you are used to the notation, it is much easier to compare these rather formal statements, and to see what the important aspects are.

These distinctive features allow each segment to be regarded as a simultaneously articulated set, or matrix, of binary features, as shown in (4).

(4)   /p/   /z/   /l/

$$
\begin{bmatrix}
-\text{voice} \\
-\text{nasal} \\
+\text{labial} \\
-\text{alveolar} \\
+\text{stop} \\
-\text{fricative} \\
-\text{approximant} \\
+\text{central}
\end{bmatrix}
\quad
\begin{bmatrix}
+\text{voice} \\
-\text{nasal} \\
-\text{labial} \\
+\text{alveolar} \\
-\text{stop} \\
+\text{fricative} \\
-\text{approximant} \\
+\text{central}
\end{bmatrix}
\quad
\begin{bmatrix}
+\text{voice} \\
-\text{nasal} \\
-\text{labial} \\
+\text{alveolar} \\
-\text{stop} \\
-\text{fricative} \\
+\text{approximant} \\
-\text{central}
\end{bmatrix}
$$

These features, however, are not entirely satisfactory. They do describe phonetic characteristics of sounds; but we are trying to provide a phonological description, not a phonetic one, and one interesting phonological fact is that features and phonemes fall into classes. For instance, the matrices in (4) have to include values for all three of the features [stop], [fricative] and [approximant], despite the fact that any sound can be only one of these. Together, they provide a classification for manner of articulation; but (4) lists them all as if they were as independent as [nasal], [voice] and [alveolar]. Similarly, in (4) values are given for [labial] and [alveolar], and we would have to add [labio-dental], [dental], [postalveolar], [palatal], [velar] and [glottal] for English alone: but again, it is simply not possible for a single consonant to be both labio-dental or velar, for instance, or both alveolar and labial. We are missing the generalisation that together, this group of features makes up the dimension of place of articulation.

One possible way of overcoming this lack of economy in the feature system is to group sets of features together, and write redundancy rules to show which values can be predicted. Redundancy rules take the shape shown in (5).

(5) [+stop]   →   [−fricative, −approximant]
      [+fricative]   →   [−stop, −approximant]
      [+labial]   →   [−labiodental, −dental, −alveolar, −palatal ...]
      [+alveolar]   →   [−labial, −labiodental, −dental, −palatal ...]

The first rule says 'if a segment is a stop, it cannot also be either a fricative or an approximant'. All these redundancy rules are universal − that is, they hold for all human languages, and are in a sense statements of logical possibilities. Particular languages may also rule out combinations of features which are theoretically possible, and which may occur routinely in many other languages. Two language-specific redundancy rules for English are given in (6): the first tells us that English has no palatal nasal (although Italian and French do), and the second, that English has only lateral approximants (though Welsh, for instance, has also a lateral fricative). These redundancy rules cannot be written the other way around: it would not be accurate to say that non-palatals are all nasal in English, or that all approximants are lateral.

(6) [+nasal]   →   [−palatal]
      [+lateral]   →   [+approximant]

While we should expect to have to state redundancy rules of the sort in (6), since these express quirks of particular languages, it seems unfortunate that our feature system is not structured so as to factor out the universal redundancies in (5). However, to produce a better phonological feature system, we first need to spell out what we want such a system to achieve.

4.4 A more economical feature system

Some requirements of a phonological feature system are as follows:

* the system should be relatively economical
* it should enlighten us about which combinations of features can go together universally, and therefore which segments and segment-types are universally possible. That is, many universal redundancy rules of the sort in (5) should not have to be written explicitly, as they will follow from the feature system.

- it should allow us to group together those segments and segment-
types which characteristically behave similarly in the world's
languages.

Certain elementary phonetic features can be adopted without further
question into our revised system: for instance, [±oral], [±lateral] and
[±voice] do correspond to binary oppositions, and help us to distinguish
classes of consonants in English and other languages. The main problems involve place and manner of articulation.

Turning first to manner of articulation, we might initially wish any
sensible feature system to distinguish vowels from consonants. This is a
division of which we are all intuitively aware, although that awareness
may owe something to written as well as spoken language. Children
learn early that, in the English alphabet, the vowel letters are <a e i o u>,
though these, alone and in combination, can signal a much larger
number of vowel sounds. When challenged to write a word 'without
vowels', English speakers might respond with *spy* or *fly*, but not *type*,
although the <y> in all three cases indicates the vowel [aɪ], while the
<e> in *type* does not correspond to a vowel in speech (or indeed, to
anything at all). Nonetheless, there is a general awareness that vowels
and consonants form different categories integral to phonology and
phonetics – an assumption central to the organisation of this book, where
the two classes are introduced in different chapters.

This binary opposition between vowels and consonants is not entirely
clear-cut. For instance, vowels are almost always voiced: it is highly
unusual for languages to have phonemically voiceless vowels, and those
that do always have voiced ones too. However, there are also consonants
which are almost always voiced: this is true of nasals, and also of approximants (like English /j w l r/). We might say that these consonants are
closer to vowels than stops and fricatives, which can be either voiced or
voiceless, and indeed often occur in pairs distinguished only by [+voice]
– think of English /p b/, /t d/, /k g/, /f v/, /s z/.

Similarly, vowels, as we shall see in Chapter 9, form the essential,
central part of syllables: it is possible to have a syllable consisting only of
a vowel, as in *I* (or *eye*), *a*, *oh*, but consonants appear at syllable margins,
preceding or following vowels, as in *sigh*, *side*, *at*, *dough*. Nonetheless,
some consonants may become syllabic under certain circumstances.
Nasals and approximants can be syllabic in English: for instance, in the
second syllables of *button*, *bottom*, *little* (and *father*, for speakers who have
an [ɹ] there), there is no vowel, only a syllabic consonant. You may think
you are producing a vowel, probably partly because there is a vowel
graph in the spelling; but in fact most speakers will move straight from

one consonant to the next, although the syllabic consonant has its own phonetic character. In IPA notation, this is signalled by a small vertical line under the consonant symbol, giving [bʌtn̩], [bɒtm̩], [lɪtl̩], [faðɹ̩]. It is not possible for oral stops and fricatives to become syllabic in this way: in *lifted*, or *horses*, there *must* be a vowel before the final [d] or [z].

This evidence seems to suggest that, on the one hand, we should distinguish all consonants from vowels. On the other hand, in many phonological processes in many different languages, the class of stops and fricatives behaves differently from the class of vowels, nasals, and approximant consonants, so that these two categories should be distinguishable too. Since these classifications cross-cut one another, it is clearly not possible to get the right results using a single binary feature, or indeed using any features proposed so far. For example, although we could describe the class of nasals, vowels and approximants as [−stop, −fricative], a negative definition of this kind does not really explain why they form a class, or what they have in common.

Many phonologists would use three features, the so-called major class features, to produce these classifications. First, we can distinguish consonants from vowels using the feature [±syllabic]; sounds which are [+syllabic] form the core, or nucleus, of a syllable, while [−syllabic] sounds form syllabic margins. Vowels are therefore [+syllabic], and all consonants [−syllabic], though some consonants (like English /m n l r/) may have [+syllabic] allophones in certain contexts. Second, the feature [±consonantal] distinguishes [+consonantal] oral stops, fricatives, nasals and 'liquids' (the cover term for /r/ and /l/ sounds), from [−consonantal] glides (like English /j/, /w/) and vowels. The crucial distinction here is an articulatory one: in [+consonantal] sounds, the airflow is obstructed in the oral cavity, either being stopped completely, or causing local audible friction; whereas for [−consonantal] sounds, airflow is continuous and unimpeded (remember that for nasal stops, although airflow continues uninterrupted through the nose, there is a complete closure in the oral cavity). Finally, [±sonorant] distinguishes nasals, vowels and all approximants from oral stops and fricatives; the former set, the sonorants, are characteristically voiced, while the latter, the obstruents, may be either voiced or voiceless.

As (7) shows, the combination of these three binary features actually distinguishes four major classes of segments.

(7) All vowels   [+syllabic, −consonantal, +sonorant]
     Glides (English /j w/)   [−syllabic, −consonantal, +sonorant]
     Liquids and nasals (sonorant
     consonants)   [−syllabic, +consonantal, +sonorant]

Oral stops and fricatives
(obstruent consonants)   [−syllabic, +consonantal, −sonorant]

However, we can produce further, flexible groupings, to reflect the fact that composite categories often behave in the same way phonologically. For example, vowels, nasals and all approximants are [+sonorant]; vowels and glides alone are [−consonantal]; and we can divide our earlier, intuitive classes of consonants and vowels using [±syllabic].

The introduction of these major class features resolves some of our earlier difficulties with manner of articulation; but we are still not able to distinguish stops from affricates or fricatives. To finish the job of accounting for manner, we must introduce two further features. The more important of these is [±continuant], which separates the oral and nasal stops, which are [−continuant] and have airflow stopped in the oral tract, from all other sounds, which are [+continuant] and have continuous oral airflow throughout their production. Second, the affricates /tʃ/ and /dʒ/ (which we have rather been ignoring up to now) can be classified as a subtype of oral plosive; but the complete articulatory closure, for these sounds only, is released more gradually than usual, so that the affricates incorporate a fricative phase. The affricates are generally described as [+delayed release], while other stops are [−delayed release].

Despite these advances in dealing with manner of articulations, there remain problems with place. Recall that, if all places of articulation are stated independently, a consonant which is [+alveolar] will also have to be listed as [−labial], [−dental], [−palatal], [−velar], and so on. To illustrate this problem, consider the different phonetic shapes of the prefix *un-* in (8).

(8) unarmed   [n]
     unpleasant   [m]
     unfavourable   [ɱ]
     unthinkable   [n̪]
     unstable   [n]
     uncomplicated [ŋ]

The prefix consonant is always nasal, but its place of articulation alters depending on the following segment. Before a vowel or an alveolar consonant, like [s], the nasal is alveolar; before a bilabial consonant like [p], it is bilabial; before a labio-dental like [f], it is labio-dental [ɱ]; before a dental, it is dental [n̪]; and before a velar, in this case [k], it is also velar. We can write these generalisations as a series of phonological rules, as in (9). These rules have the same format as the redundancy rules proposed above; but instead of stating generalisations about necessary combinations of features, or excluded combinations, they summarise processes which take place in the structure of a particular language, in a certain context.

(9)
$$\begin{bmatrix} +\text{nasal} \\ +\text{alveolar} \\ -\text{labial} \\ -\text{dental} \\ -\text{velar} \end{bmatrix} \rightarrow \begin{bmatrix} -\text{alveolar} \\ +\text{labial} \end{bmatrix} \quad / \underline{\hspace{1cm}} [+\text{labial}]$$

$$\begin{bmatrix} +\text{nasal} \\ +\text{alveolar} \\ -\text{dental} \\ -\text{labial} \\ -\text{velar} \end{bmatrix} \rightarrow \begin{bmatrix} -\text{alveolar} \\ +\text{dental} \end{bmatrix} \quad / \underline{\hspace{1cm}} [+\text{dental}]$$

$$\begin{bmatrix} +\text{nasal} \\ +\text{alveolar} \\ -\text{velar} \\ -\text{labial} \\ -\text{dental} \end{bmatrix} \rightarrow \begin{bmatrix} -\text{alveolar} \\ +\text{velar} \end{bmatrix} \quad / \underline{\hspace{1cm}} [+\text{velar}]$$

... and so on

In these rules, the material furthest left is the input to the process, or what we start with – nasals with different place features in each case. The arrow means 'becomes', or technically 'is rewritten as'; and there then follows a specification of the change that takes place. In (9), this always involves changing the place of articulation. Any feature which is not explicitly mentioned in the middle section of the statement is taken to be unchanged; so in the first rule, the consonant involved stays [+nasal, −dental, −velar], but changes its values for [±alveolar] and [±labial]. The rest of the statement following the environment bar / (which can be paraphrased as 'in the following environment') specifies the context where this particular realisation appears. In (9), the environment always involves a following sound with a particular place of articulation: the line signals where the input fits into the sequence.

The problem is that this system of features, with several different places of articulation each expressed using a different feature, will lead to gross duplication in the statement of what is, in fact, a rather simple and straightforward generalisation: /n/ comes to share the place of articulation of the following consonant. What seems to matter here is that the place of articulation of the output matches that of the con-ditioning context. If we were to regard all the place features as subdivisions of a higher-order feature 'place', we could state the whole rule as in (10).

(10) $\begin{bmatrix} +\text{nasal} \\ +\text{alveolar} \end{bmatrix} \rightarrow \quad [\alpha \text{ place}] \quad / \underline{\quad\quad} [\alpha \text{ place}]$

This rule tells us that the place of articulation of the input consonant, an alveolar nasal, comes to match the place of the following segment, using a Greek letter variable. If the output and conditioning context also matched in voicing and nasality, for instance, further Greek letter variables could be introduced, so that the output and context would be specified as [α place, β voice, γ nasal]. A more advanced subpart of phonology, feature geometry, investigates which features might be characterised as variants of a superordinate feature like 'place' in this way.

Although recognising a superordinate 'place' feature allows an economical statement of this particular process, we also need a way of referring to each individual place of articulation: after all, not all consonants will always undergo all rules in the same way, and indeed the input of (10) is still restricted to the alveolar nasal. It seems we must reject features like [±alveolar], [±velar], and turn again to a more economical, phonological feature set, which ideally should also help us group together those places of articulation which typically behave similarly cross-linguistically.

One generally accepted solution involves the two features [±anterior] and [±coronal]. [+anterior] sounds are those where the passive articulator is the alveolar ridge or further forward; this includes labial, labio-dental, dental and alveolar sounds. [−anterior] sounds are produced further back in the vocal tract; for English, this will include postalveolar, palatal, velar and glottal sounds (and also, note, the labial-velars /w/ and /ʍ/). For [+coronal] sounds, the active articulator is the tip, blade or front of the tongue, so including dental, alveolar, postalveolar and palatal consonants in English; conversely, [−coronal] sounds, such as labials, labio-dentals, labial-velars, velars and glottals, do not involve the front parts of the tongue. This system is undoubtedly economical, even though we require one further feature, [±strident], to distinguish fricatives like /s/ from /θ/: these will both be [−syllabic, +consonantal, −sonorant, +anterior, +coronal] in the feature system developed so far. [+strident] sounds in English are [f v s z ʃ ʒ tʃ dʒ].

Rule (11) applies these features to English [k] and [c]. Note that it is common practice to exclude features which are not absolutely necessary to distinguish the sound or sounds referred to from others in the language: thus, although the input /k/ is strictly also [−nasal, −lateral, −delayed release, −strident], these redundant feature values need not be included, as /k/ is already uniquely identified from the features given.

(11)
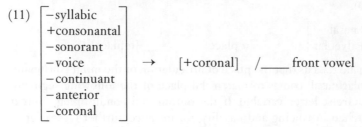

$$
\begin{bmatrix}
-\text{syllabic} \\
+\text{consonantal} \\
-\text{sonorant} \\
-\text{voice} \\
-\text{continuant} \\
-\text{anterior} \\
-\text{coronal}
\end{bmatrix}
\rightarrow \quad [+\text{coronal}] \quad /\underline{\quad} \text{ front vowel}
$$

Ideally, the explanation for the presence of a certain allophone in a certain context should be available in the rule itself. In (11), however, /k/ becomes [+coronal] before a front vowel; but the connection between [coronal] and [front] is obscured by the different descriptions conventionally used for vowels and consonants. We return to vowel features in Chapters 6 and 7.

4.5 Natural classes

The major class features identify several categories of sounds which recur cross-linguistically in different phonological rules. Feature notation can also show why certain sounds behave similarly in similar contexts, within these larger classes. For instance, English /p/, /t/ and /k/ aspirate at the beginnings of words. All three may also be glottally reinforced at the ends of words. All three are unaspirated after /s/; and no other English phoneme has the same range of allophones, in the same environments. In feature terms, although /p/, /t/, /k/ differ in place of articulation, all three are obstruent consonants, and within this class, are [−voice, −nasal, −continuant]. A group of phonemes which show the same behaviour in the same contexts, and which share the same features, constitute a natural class. More formally, a natural class of phonemes can be identified using a smaller number of features than any individual member of that class. As (12) shows, the class of voiceless plosives, /p/, /t/ and /k/, can be defined uniquely using only three features. If we subtract one of the plosives, we need more features, since we must then specify the place of articulation; and the same is true in defining a single plosive unambiguously.

(12)   /p t k/   /p t/   /p/

$$
\begin{bmatrix}
-\text{voice} \\
-\text{nasal} \\
-\text{continuant}
\end{bmatrix}
\qquad
\begin{bmatrix}
-\text{voice} \\
-\text{nasal} \\
-\text{continuant} \\
+\text{anterior}
\end{bmatrix}
\qquad
\begin{bmatrix}
-\text{voice} \\
-\text{nasal} \\
-\text{continuant} \\
+\text{anterior} \\
-\text{coronal}
\end{bmatrix}
$$

Phonological rules very typically affect natural classes of phonemes. For example, medial voicing of /f/ to [v] in Old English, discussed briefly in Chapter 2, did not only affect that labial fricative, but also the other members of the voiceless fricative class, /s/ and /θ/. If we wrote a rule for /f/ alone, it would have to exclude the other voiceless fricatives, so that the input would have to include [+anterior, −coronal]; however, the more general fricative voicing rule in (13) requires fewer features to characterise the input, as we would expect when a natural class is involved.

(13) $\begin{bmatrix} +\text{continuant} \\ +\text{consonantal} \\ -\text{voice} \end{bmatrix}$ → [+voice] / [+voice]___[+voice]

This rule also neatly captures the connection between the process and its conditioning context, and therefore shows the motivation for the development: the fricatives, which are generally voiceless, becomes voiced between voiced sounds. This will often mean between vowels, as in *heofon* and *hlaford*; but it may also mean between a vowel and a voiced consonant, as in *hæfde*. If voicing takes place between voiced sounds, instead of having to switch off vocal fold vibration for a single segment and then switch it back on again, the vocal folds can continue vibrating through the whole sequence. Voicing the fricative in this context is therefore another example of assimilation, where one sound is influenced by another close to it in the utterance.

4.6 A warning note on phonological rules

Paradoxically, phonological rules are *not* rules in one of the common, everyday English meanings of that word; they are not regulations, which spell out what *must* happen. Instead, they are formal descriptions of what *does* happen, for speakers of a particular variety of a particular language at a particular time. Some phonological rules may also state what *sometimes* happens, with the outcome depending on issues outside phonology and phonetics altogether. For example, if you say *hamster* slowly and carefully, it will sound like [hamstə] (or [hamstəɹ], depending on whether you 'drop your [r]s' in this context or not: we return to this issue in Chapter 8, and to vowels in Chapters 6 and 7, so don't worry too much about the vowel symbols for now). If you say the word quickly several times, you will produce something closer to your normal, casual speech pronunciation, and it is highly likely that there will be an extra consonant in there, giving [hampstə] (or [hampstəɹ] instead. As the rate of speech increases, adjacent sounds influence one another even more than usual, because the same complex articulations are taking place in even less time. Here, the articulators are moving from a voiced nasal stop [m], to a voiceless alveolar fricative [s], so that almost every possible property has to change all at once (apart from the source and direction of the airstream, which all English sounds have in common anyway). In fast speech, not all these transitions may be perfectly coordinated: the extraneous [p] appears when the speaker has succeeded in switching off voicing, and raising the velum to cut off airflow through the nose, but has not yet shifted from stop to fricative, or from labial to alveolar. There is consequently a brief moment when the features appropriate for [p] are all in place, before the place and manner of articulation are also altered to produce the intended [s]. Listing the feature composition of [m], [p] and [s], as in (14), reveals that [p] shares half the features of each of [m] and [s], so it is entirely understandable that [p] should arise from this casual speech process.

(14)

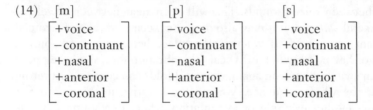

$$\begin{matrix} [m] \\ \begin{bmatrix} +\text{voice} \\ -\text{continuant} \\ +\text{nasal} \\ +\text{anterior} \\ -\text{coronal} \end{bmatrix} \end{matrix} \quad \begin{matrix} [p] \\ \begin{bmatrix} -\text{voice} \\ -\text{continuant} \\ -\text{nasal} \\ +\text{anterior} \\ -\text{coronal} \end{bmatrix} \end{matrix} \quad \begin{matrix} [s] \\ \begin{bmatrix} -\text{voice} \\ +\text{continuant} \\ -\text{nasal} \\ +\text{anterior} \\ +\text{coronal} \end{bmatrix} \end{matrix}$$

A very similar process arises in words like *mince* and *prince*, which can become homophonous (that is, identical in sound) to *mints* and *prints* in fast speech. Here, the transition is from [n], a voiced alveolar nasal stop, to [s], a voiceless alveolar oral fricative, and the half-way house is [t], which this time shares its place of articulation with both neighbours, but differs from [n] in voicing and nasality, and from [s] in manner of articulation. In both *hamster* and *mince/prince*, however, the casual speech process creating the extra medial plosive is an optional one. This does not mean that it is consciously controlled by the speaker: but the formality of the situation, the identity of the person you are talking to, and even the topic of conversation can determine how likely these casual speech processes are. In a formal style, for instance asking a question after a lecture, or having a job interview, you are far more likely to make a careful transition from nasal to fricative in words of this kind, while informal style, for instance chatting to friends over a drink, is much more conducive to intrusion of the 'extra' plosive. These issues of formality and social context, which are the domain of sociolinguistics, are not directly within the scope of phonetics and phonology, although they clearly influence speakers' phonetic and phonological behaviour.

If speakers of English keep pronouncing [hampstə] and [prɪnts] *prince* in sufficient numbers, and in enough contexts, these pronunciations may become the norm, extending even into formal circumstances, and being learned as the canonical pronunciation by children (this is exactly what has already happened in *bramble*, and the name *Dempster*). Even now, children (and occasionally adults too) spell *hamster* as *hampster*, showing that they may believe this to be the 'correct' form. Developments from casual to formal pronunciation are one source of language change, and mean that phonological rules and systems can vary between languages, and can change over time. For instance, as we saw earlier, modern English has a phonemic contrast between /f/ and /v/, but in Old English, [f] and [v] were allophones of a single phoneme, /f/.

No feature system is perfect; however carefully designed a system is, it will not in itself explain all the properties of a particular language, which may sometimes reflect quirks and idiosyncrasies which have arisen during the history of that system. Equally, some developments of one sound into another are perfectly natural in a particular context, but the feature system fails to express this transparently because it is so closely linked to articulation: voiceless sonorants are rare simply because they are rather difficult to hear, and the best possible features, if they lack an acoustic aspect, will fail to reflect that fact. Just as we are all speakers and hearers, so sounds have both articulatory and acoustic components: sometimes one of these is relevant in determining allophonic variation, sometimes the other – and sometimes both. For instance, it is quite common cross-linguistically for labial sounds, like [p] or [f], to turn into velar ones, like [k] or [x], and vice versa: in words like *cough*, the <gh> originally signalled a velar fricative, [x], which has historically become [f]. In articulatory terms, labials and velars have little in common: indeed, they are produced almost at opposite ends of the vocal tract. We can at least use [−coronal] for the composite set of labials and velars; but this would also, counterfactually, include glottals; and in any case, negative definitions are of limited usefulness (why should two classes of consonants work together because both do *not* involve the front of the tongue?). However, acoustic analysis reveals a striking similarity in the profile of energy making up labials and velars, so that the two categories are heard as more similar than we might expect. In addition, the vowel in *cough* is pronounced with rounded lips; if this lip-rounding is carried on just a little too long, so that it affects the following consonant, the articulators will also be in a position appropriate for [f]. In this case, articulatory and acoustic factors have worked together to change the [x] of earlier English to the [f] we find today. Most phonological feature systems are based uniquely either on articulatory or on acoustic factors: either way, we would miss part of the story in a case like this.

However, adopting a feature system of one sort or another is invaluable in formalising phonological rules; in sharpening up our thinking when formulating such rules; in seeing segments like [p] or [s] as shorthand for a bundle of properties, rather than as mysterious, self-contained units; and in trying to explain why certain sounds and groups of sounds behave in the way they do. Despite some limitations, the feature system outlined above will therefore be used in the rest of this book.

Exercises

1. In Exercise 1 of Chapter 2, you were presented with the following pronunciations, from a learner of English as a second language.

that [dat]	dog [dɒg]	head [hɛd]
leather [lɛðə]	leader [liːðə]	
sing [ʃɪŋ]	sat [sat]	loss [lɒs]
fish [fɪʃ]	miss [mɪʃ]	push [pus]

Write rules accounting for the distribution of the allophones of /d/ (= [d] and [ð]), and /s/ (= [s] and [ʃ]), using binary features. Note that the symbol for a word boundary is #; so if a process takes place at the beginning of a word, we write / # ____ as the environment, and likewise / ____ # for the end.

2. The following data appeared in Exercise 3 of Chapter 2. State the distribution of the voiced and voiceless allophones of /b/, /z/ and /g/ as economically as possible. How many rules do you need?

pronunciation	meaning
[bim]	'rug'
[bin]	'head'
[zak]	'parrot'
[zip]	'ostrich'
[azaŋ]	'to speak'
[obas]	'to throw'
[mohis]	'to eat'
[zigah]	'to sing'
[gik]	'ant'
[gah]	'a song'
[nagok]	'to sting'
[habis]	'to drink'

3. Produce feature matrices, including *all* the features introduced in this chapter, for the following English sounds: /l r p d s θ ŋ ʤ w/.

4. In your matrices for Exercise 3, put brackets round the redundant features; that is, those which do not have to be included for the segment to be uniquely identified. In some cases, you may notice general patterns; if so, state these as redundancy rules.

5. In each of the following lists, the sounds involved constitute a natural class for English, except that there is one odd sound. Find the odd one out in each case, and define the natural class using features.

   (a) [l ɹ b j w]
   (b) [p g k ð d b t]
   (c) [k n s t l d ɹ z]

6. Sequences of consonants, such as those at the beginning of *train, stray, fly,* are known as consonant clusters. In two-consonant clusters which have [s] as the first consonant, what can the second consonant be? Can these consonants be grouped into a natural class or several natural classes? In three-consonant clusters which have [s] as the first consonant, what can the second and third consonants be? Can these consonants be grouped into a natural class or several natural classes?

Recommendations for reading

Giegerich (1992) provides a clear and detailed overview of distinctive features of the sort introduced here, with special emphasis on English. Consideration of features and feature theory, and the mechanics of rule-writing, is also included in most recent general textbooks on phonology, including Carr (1993), Durand (1990), Katamba (1988), Spencer (1996). Lass (1984) provides a particularly helpful critique of some elements of feature theory, including binarity and the emphasis on articulation. The features used here are ultimately derived from Chomsky and Halle (1968), although this is not an easy book for beginners, and should be approached with caution!

5 Criteria for contrast: the phoneme system

5.1 Minimal pairs and beyond

The main business of the last chapter was the construction of rules stating allophonic distributions. These rules in turn were based on the identification of phonemes, for which we relied on the two fundamental tools of predictability of occurrence and invariance of meaning: if two sounds occur in non-overlapping, predictable sets of contexts, and if substituting one for the other does not make a semantic difference, then those two sounds must necessarily be allophones of a single phoneme. On the other hand, if those two sounds can occur in the same environments, producing different words, they belong to different phonemes. This diagnosis is confirmed by the commutation test, which involves putting different sounds in a particular context, to see if minimal pairs result. An example for English consonants is given in (1).

(1) *Context:*   *-at*

pat	/p/
bat	/b/
mat	/m/
fat	/f/
vat	/v/
that	/ð/
tat	/t/
sat	/s/
gnat	/n/
rat	/r/
chat	/ʧ/
cat	/k/
hat	/h/

Accidental gaps in the English vocabulary mean that no lexical item *jat*, or *lat*, or *dat* is available. However, minimal pairs can be found in slightly different contexts to establish /ʤ/, /l/, /g/ and so on as consonant phonemes of English: hence, we find *sip zip dip tip lip*, or *cot dot shot jot*. Considering a range of contexts provides evidence for all the consonant phonemes of English, which are plotted on a chart in (2): the voiceless labial-velar and velar fricatives /ʍ/ and /x/ appear in brackets because they are found only in some varieties of English.

(2)

	labial	labio-dental	dental	alveolar	post alveolar	palatal	velar	glottal
plosive	p b			t d			k g	
nasal	m			n			ŋ	
affricate					tʃ dʒ			
fricative	(ʍ)	f v	θ ð	s z	ʃ ʒ		(x)	h
approximant	w			l r		j		

Minimal pairs and the commutation test alone will generally suffice to establish the members of a phoneme system: according to Charles Hockett, a mid-twentieth century American linguist who was very influential in the development of phoneme theory, 'Minimal pairs are the analyst's delight, and he seeks them whenever there is any hope of finding them'. However, there are some circumstances where phonemes cannot be established by minimal pairs alone, and we need supplementary criteria for phonemicisation, or phonological units above and beyond the phoneme. In the sections below, we turn to these special cases, and also to a consideration of the phoneme system itself, and its relevance and reality for language users.

5.2 Phonetic similarity and defective distributions

5.2.1 Phonetic similarity

In the vast majority of cases, applying our phoneme tests will provide results in keeping with native speakers' intuitions about which sounds belong together; very often, as we have seen, allophones of a single phoneme will not in fact be distinguishable for a native speaker at all, without a certain amount of phonetic training. However, there are some cases where sticking to those tests too rigidly can have quite the opposite consequence.

One of the best-known and most obvious examples of this kind in English involves [h] and [ŋ]. The minimal pairs in (5.1) show that [h] contrasts with a number of English consonant phonemes word-initially; but there is no minimal pair for [ŋ]. Conversely, in word-final position, it is straightforward to find contrasts for [ŋ], as in *rang, ran, ram, rat, rack, rag, rap, rash*; but there is no equivalent minimal pair for [h]. The generalisation extractable from this is that [h] appears only before a stressed vowel (or at the beginning of a syllable; see Chapter 9), as in *hat, ahead, apprehensive, vehicular* (but not *vehicle*, where <h> appears in the spelling, but there is no [h], as the stress here falls on the first vowel). On the other hand, [ŋ] is not permissible syllable-initially: it can appear only at the end of a syllable, either alone, as in *rang, hanger*, or before a velar plosive, either [k] or [g], as in *rink, stinker, finger, stronger*.

What this means, in purely technical terms, is that [h] and [ŋ] are in complementary distribution. One appears only syllable-initially, where the other never does; and in consequence, there is no possible minimal pair which will distinguish the two. If we take only predictability of occurrence and invariance of meaning into account, we will be forced into setting up a phoneme which we might symbolise as /ɧ/, which is realised as [h] in one set of environments, and [ŋ] in another.

It is not going to be easy to convince native speakers of English that this is the right solution − not because we have to work on bringing previously subconscious intuitions to the surface, but because those intuitions suggest strongly that [h] and [ŋ] are entirely separate and unrelated. There is some evidence in favour of that view, too. First, although we have seen that the English spelling system is not absolutely and reliably phonemic, different spellings are never consistently used for different allophones of a single phoneme, as would be the case for [h] <h> and [ŋ] <ng> / <nk>. Second, native speakers can easily tell the two sounds apart, which would not be true, for instance, of clear and dark variants of /l/, or aspirated and unaspirated allophones of /p/. Since our core criteria for allophony very generally give the right results, it is prob-ably unwise to mess about with them much; but we can add a further condition on determining allophony, which applies both to the 'normal' cases and to the situation of [h] and [ŋ].

In brief, this additional criterion for allophony states that all the allo-phones of a phoneme must be phonetically similar. Using distinctive features allows this rather vague notion to be quantified: but there is still no straightforward equation for determining what counts as phonetically similar and what does not. However, although we cannot draw a dividing line which will be universally applicable, for instance requiring that the allophones of a single phoneme must be different by no more than three features, we might at least hypothesise that two sounds are highly unlikely to be allophones of the same phoneme if the number of con-trasting feature values is higher than the number of shared ones. For [h] and [ŋ], this produces an unambiguous result: both are consonants, but there the similarity ends. [h] is a voiceless fricative, while [ŋ] is a voiced stop; [h] is oral, while [ŋ] is nasal; [h] is glottal, while [ŋ] is velar; [h] is an obstruent, while [ŋ] is a sonorant. On almost every parameter which could distinguish the two, they are in fact distinct. Rather than setting up a single phoneme with two such bizarrely different realisations, invoking phonetic similarity allows us to justify regarding /h/ and /ŋ/ as distinct phonemes, despite the lack of minimal pairs.

Phonetic similarity also helps in cases where a single allophone could theoretically be assigned to more than one possible phoneme, a situation commonly encountered when members of a natural class of phonemes undergo the same rule. For instance, we have seen that in Old English, the voiceless fricatives /f θ s/ were voiced between voiced sounds. It follows that all the voiceless fricative allophones were in complementary distribution with all the voiced ones, since [v ð z] could appear only between voiced sounds, and [f θ s] could appear only elsewhere. Purely on the grounds of predictability of occurrence and invariance of meaning, there is no guidance on which of these we should assign to which phoneme: in theory we could set up one phoneme with allophones [f] and [z], a second with [θ] and [v], and a third with [s] and [ð], if all that matters is for one allophone to be voiceless and the other to be voiced. We might also feel that this solution would make Old English speakers turn in their graves: their intuitions are highly likely to have favoured grouping the two labial sounds together, the two dentals, and the two alveolars. Again, this intuitive solution is supported by a requirement of phonetic similarity, this time involving the assignment of the two most similar allophones, those sharing a place of articulation, to a single phoneme in each case. In Modern English, a precisely similar problem and solution arise with the voiceless stop phonemes and their aspirated and unaspirated allophones.

5.2.2 Defective distribution

Of course, if /h/ and /ŋ/ were entirely normal phonemes, we would not have got into the problematic situation of regarding them as potential realisations of the same phoneme in the first place. In the normal case, we would expect some realisation of every phoneme in a language to appear in every possible environment: initially, medially, and finally in the word, and also before and after other consonants in clusters. There are, however, two types of exception to this sweeping generalisation.

First, there are the phonotactic constraints of a language, which spell out which combinations of sounds are possible. In English, as we saw in the exercises to the last chapter, only rather few three-consonant clusters are permissible; and the first consonant in the sequence must always be /s/. Nasal stops in English can cluster only with oral stops sharing the same place of articulation (unless the oral stop marks the past tense, as in *harmed*); hence *lamp, clamber, plant, land, rink, finger*, but not **lamk, *lanp*, *[laŋt]. Even more specifically, /v/ and /m/ cannot be the first member of *any* initial consonant cluster, although both can occur alone initially, medially and finally; and /h/ never clusters at all (although, again, this was possible in Old English, where there are forms like *hring* 'ring', *hwæl* 'whale'). Phonotactic statements of this kind restrict the length and composition of possible clusters, on a language-specific (and period-specific) basis.

Secondly, some phonemes have defective distributions: they are not only restricted in the combinations of consonants they can form, but are simply absent from some positions in the word. English /h/ and /ŋ/ both fall into this category, since the former is available only syllable-initially, and the latter only syllable-finally. It is because those defective distributions are mutually exclusive that English [h] and [ŋ] are in complementary distribution.

Phonemes with defective distributions like this are relatively rare. Sometimes, their defectiveness follows from their historical development: [ŋ] is derived historically from a sequence of [nk] or [ng] where the nasal assimilated to the place of articulation of the following consonant; and since initial clusters of nasal plus stop are not permissible in earlier English or today, the appropriate context for [ŋ] never arose word-initially. Similarly, a chain of sound changes leading to the weakening and loss of /h/ before consonants and word-finally has left it 'stranded' only syllable-initially before a vowel; and there is a parallel story in non-rhotic varieties of English, where /r/ is pronounced before a vowel, but not before a consonant or a pause, meaning that [ɹ] appears in *red, bread, very*, but not in *dark, car*. Often, defectively distributed phonemes are relatively new arrivals. For instance, the newest member of the English consonant system is probably /ʒ/, which developed in Middle and Early Modern English from sequences of [zj] in *measure, treasure*, and from French loans such as *rouge, beige*: the [zj] sequence does not appear word-initially, and although French does allow [ʒ] here, as in *jamais* 'never', no words with that structure have been borrowed into English, leading to an apparent prohibition on word-initial English [ʒ] which is really accidental, and may change in time (as suggested by recent loans like *gîte*).

5.3 Free variation

The previous section dealt with an exception to the criterion of predictability of occurrence: two sounds which are in complementary distribution are normally assigned to a single phoneme, but where this would conflict with phonetic similarity (and with native speakers' intuitions), it is appropriate to set up two distinct phonemes and seek an alternative explanation for the complementarity, in terms of defective distributions. In this section, we turn to an exception to the other main criterion for allophony, invariance of meaning.

When one sound is substituted for another and no meaning difference arises, we are dealing with two allophones of the same phoneme. An English speaker who produces a dark [ɫ] in initial position may be regarded as having an unfamiliar accent, or some sort of minor speech impediment, but there is little danger that *light* pronounced with initial [ɫ] is going to be mistaken for another word entirely.

However, sometimes there is more than one possible pronunciation in the same word or context; this is known as free variation, and raises two possible theoretical problems. First, we require complementary distribution to assign two sounds to a single phoneme; and yet a speaker of Scottish English, for example, may sometimes produce a tapped allophone of /r/ in *very*, and on other occasions, an approximant. There are no possible minimal pairs for tapped [r] versus approximant [ɹ], and an allophonic rule can indeed be written, such that the tap appears intervocalically, as in *very*, and the approximant word-initially and word-finally. Apparent exceptions are sociolinguistically motivated: perhaps the Scot is talking to an English English speaker, who will typically not use the tap, and is subconsciously accommodating her speech towards that of her interlocutor; perhaps she is trying to sound less like a Scot; perhaps she is in a very formal situation, where more standard pronunciations are favoured. Clearly, such stylistic variation is not free in sociolinguistic terms, though it is known as free variation phonologically because there is no watertight phonological or phonetic context determining the appearance of one allophone rather than the other. The variable appearance of a glottal stop or [t] medially in *butter*, for instance, would fall into the same category, and the frequency of occurrence of the two variants would be subject to explanation in the same sociolinguistic terms.

The second type of free variation is the converse of the first, and potentially more problematic. Here, instead of finding two allophones of a single phoneme in the same context, violating complementary distribution, we see two sounds which on other criteria belong to different phonemes, failing to make the meaning difference we expect. Sometimes the difference can be explained in geographical terms: for instance, Southern British English speakers say *tomahto*, and North American speakers typically say *tomayto*, producing the same lexical item with consistently different vowels. Those two vowels, [ɑ] and [eɪ] respectively, nonetheless contrast for speakers of both accents, although as we shall see in more detail in the next three chapters, they appear in different sets of words: a Southern British English speaker will have relevant minimal pairs in *psalm* and *same*, or *grass* and *grace*, while a General American speaker will contrast *lot* with *late*, or *odd* with *aid*. The two different pronunciations of *tomato* are therefore simply characteristic of speakers from different areas.

In other cases, the same speaker uses different phonemes in the same word on different occasions of utterance. Some speakers consistently pronounce *economic* with the [ɛ] of *elephant*, and others with the [i] of *eat*; but many more produce sometimes one, and sometimes the other. And yet there are plenty of minimal pairs to establish a contrast between /ɛ/ in *pet*, *hell* or *bed*, and /i/ in *peat*, *heal* or *head*, outside that single problematic lexical item. The same is true for *either* and *neither*, which some speakers produce with [i], others with the [aɪ] of *high*, and still others with variation between the two. Again, there is no question that /i/ and /aɪ/ constitute different phonemes, with minimal pairs including *he* and *high*, *heed* and *hide*, or *steal* and *stile*. This is theoretically problematic: two sounds which on all other criteria belong to different phonemes are nonetheless found in the same context without making a meaning difference, directly contravening invariance of meaning. However, such examples tend to be few and far between, and involve only single lexical items; and again, the explanation is typically sociolinguistic. These pronunciations often develop in different geographical areas, then one spreads into the territory of the other. One variant may become stigmatised, and the other fashionable; but this stylistic variation can disappear over time, leaving two rather neutral alternatives. In such cases, the resulting variation can be truly free; but as long as the phonemes involved can be identified on the basis of minimal pairs elsewhere, these can simply be regarded as one-off exceptions. They are parallel to cases where a speaker stores two words, from the same historical source but each now appropriate in a different dialect, like the Scot who uses *kirk* with fellow Scots, but otherwise *church*; or indeed, to the use of historically unrelated synonyms like *sofa* and *settee*.

5.4 Neutralisation

This second type of free variation can also be seen as constituting the tip of a much larger theoretical iceberg. In the [ɛ]*conomic* – [i]*conomic* cases, two otherwise contrastive sounds are both possible in a single word. The contrast between two phonemes may also be interrupted more systematically, in a particular phonological context; in this case, rather than the two phonemes being equally possible alternatives, we find some form intermediate between the two.

One example involves the voiceless and voiced English plosives. These seem to contrast in all possible positions in the word: minimal pairs can be found for /t/ and /d/ initially, as in *till* versus *dill;* medially, in *matter* versus *madder;* finally, as in *lit* versus *lid;* and in consonant clusters, as in *trill, font* versus *drill, fond* – and the same is true for the labial and velar plosives. However, no contrast is possible in an initial cluster, after /s/: *spill, still* and *skill* are perfectly normal English words, but there is no **sbill, *sdill* or **sgill.* This phenomenon is known as neutralisation, because the otherwise robust and regular contrast between two sets of phonemes is neutralised, or suspended, in a particular context – in this case, after /s/.

In fact, matters are slightly more complicated yet. Although the spelling might suggest that the sounds found after /s/ are realisations of the voiceless stops, we have already seen that, in one crucial respect, they do not behave as we would expect voiceless stops to behave at the beginning of a word: that is, they are not aspirated. On the other hand, they do not behave like realisations of /b d g/ either, since they are not voiced. That is to say, the whatever-it-is that appears after /s/ has something in common with both /p/ and /b/, or /t/ and /d/, or /k/ and /g/, being an oral plosive of a particular place of articulation. But in another sense, it is neither one nor the other, since it lacks aspiration, which is the distinctive phonetic characteristic of an initial voiceless stop, and it also lacks voicing, the main signature of an initial voiced one.

There are two further pieces of evidence, one practical and the other theoretical, in support of the in-between status of the sounds following /s/. If a recording is made of *spill, still, skill,* the [s] is erased, and the remaining portion is played to native speakers of English, they find it difficult to tell whether the words are *pill, till, kill,* or *bill, dill, gill.* Furthermore, we might argue that a /t/ is a /t/ because it contrasts with /d/ – phonemes are defined by the other phonemes in the system they belong to. To take an analogy, again from written English, children learning to write often have difficulty in placing the loop for a <b> right at the base of the upstroke, and it sometimes appears a little higher than in adult writing – which is fine, as long as it doesn't migrate so high as to be mistaken for a <p>, where the loop is meant to appear at the top. What matters is maintaining distinctness between the two; and the same is true in speech, where a realisation of /d/, for instance, can be more or less voiced in different circumstances, as long as it does not become confused with realisations of /t/. In a case where the two cannot possibly contrast, as after /s/ in English, /t/ cannot be defined as it normally is, precisely because here alone, it does not contrast with /d/. It follows again that the voiceless, unaspirated sound after /s/ in *still* cannot be a normal allophone of /t/.

Phonologists call the unit found in a position of neutralisation an archiphoneme. The archiphoneme is symbolised by a capital letter, and is composed of all the properties which the neutralised phonemes have in common, but not the properties which typically distinguish them, as shown in (3).

(3)   /T/

$$\begin{bmatrix} +\text{oral} \\ +\text{stop} \\ +\text{alveolar} \\ 0 \text{ voice} \end{bmatrix}$$

The archiphoneme /T/ is proposed where the normal opposition between /t/ and /d/ is suspended, so neither /t/ nor /d/ is a possibility. /T/ is an intermediate form, sharing the feature values common to /t/ and /d/, but with no value possible for voicing, since there is no contrast of voiced and voiceless in this context. Neutralisation is therefore the defective distribution of a class of phonemes, involving a particular phonological context (rather than a single word, as in the *either/neither* case).

There are many other cases of neutralisation in English, but for the time being, we shall consider only one. In many varieties of English, the normal contrasts between vowels break down before /r/. To take one example, British English speakers will tend to maintain a three-way contrast of *Mary, merry* and *marry*, whereas many speakers of General American suspend the usual contrast of /eɪ/, /ɛ/ and /æ/, as established by minimal triplets like *sail, sell* and *Sal* or *pain, pen* and *pan*, in this environment, making *Mary, merry* and *marry* homophones. Although the vowel found here often sounds like [ɛ], this cannot be regarded as a normal realisation of /ɛ/, since /ɛ/ is a phoneme which contrasts with /eɪ/ and /æ/, and that contrast is not possible here. So, we can set up an archiphoneme /E/ in just those cases before /r/, again signalling that a contrast otherwise found in all environments fails to manifest itself here.

5.5 Phonology and morphology

The archiphoneme is useful in signalling cases where oppositions are suspended, but has two problems. First, a representation like /mEri/ is three ways ambiguous for a General American speaker, since it could be *Mary, merry* or *marry*: this might in fact be quite appropriate, because the three sound the same at the phonetic level, but it would be helpful to have a way of identifying, somewhere in the phonology, just which is which. Secondly, in some cases that look rather like neutralisation, the archiphoneme cannot really be invoked. For instance, the English regular plural ending on nouns is marked by an <s> spelling, which means more than one thing phonologically: in *cats, caps, chiefs*, where the final sound of the stem is voiceless, the plural suffix is realised as voiceless [s]; in *dogs, heads, pans, hooves, dolls, eyes*, where the final sound of the stem is voiced, the plural suffix is also voiced [z]; and finally, in cases where the stem ends in a sibilant, namely [s z ʃ ʒ tʃ dʒ], a vowel is inserted for reasons of ease of articulation, since sequences of two sibilants are not allowed in English, giving *horses, bushes, churches* with [əz] (or [ɪz]). This might, on the face of it, seem to be a purely phonetic matter, involving assimilation of the plural ending to the last segment of the stem; but there is more to it than that. If voicing assimilation were necessary in final clusters, forms like *hence, face, loss* would not be possible words of English, since they involve final sequences of a voiced consonant or vowel, followed by voiceless [s]. What matters, in the plural cases, is what that final sound is doing: the cases where it is a suffix indicating plural behave differently from those in which it is part of the stem.

Similarly, singular and plural noun forms like *leaf – leaves, hoof – hooves, knife – knives* might initially appear to represent a case of neutralisation, where the usual contrast between /f/ and /v/ is suspended before /z/ (recall that this <s> is pronounced voiced). However, whatever is going on here cannot be ascribed straightforwardly to the phonetic context, since there are also cases, as in (4), where either the singular and plural both have voiceless fricatives, or both have voiced ones.

(4) chief – chiefs   roof – roofs
     hive – hives   stove – stoves

Neutralisation always involves a regular suspension of contrast in a particular phonetic context. Here, we are dealing with an alternation between two phonemes, /f/ and /v/, in a particular grammatical context. *Leaf* has a final /f/, and *leaves* a medial /v/ – there is no intermediate, archiphonemic form here. The determining factor is neither phonetic nor phonological: it is simply a fact about certain English nouns (including *leaf, hoof, knife, life, wife,* but excluding *chief, roof, hive, stove*) that they have /f/ in some forms, notably the singular, and /v/ in others, notably the plural.

Such alternation between phonemes, depending on grammatical facts, is very common. For instance, before certain suffixes, the shape of the final consonant of a stem may change: hence /k/, /s/ and /ʃ/, otherwise three distinct phonemes as in *kin, sin* and *shin*, occur predictably depending whether the stem *electric* stands alone, or has a following suffix. Similar alternations involve *president* and other words derived from that, as shown in (5). English speakers can perfectly well pronounce [k] before the sound sequence [ɪti], as in *kitty*, or [t] before [i], as in *pretty* or *Betty*: the fact that these sounds do not appear in *electricity* or *presidency*, where we find [s] instead, reflects the function of *-ity* and *-y* as suffixes in those cases.

(5) electri[k]   electri[s]ity   electri[ʃ]ian
     presiden[t]   presiden[s]y   presiden[ʃ]ial

5.6 Rules and constraints

Most interactions of phonology with morphology, the part of linguistics which studies how words are made up of meaningful units, like stems and suffixes, are beyond the scope of this book, although the overlap between the two areas, commonly known as morphophonemics, has been extremely important in the development of phonological theory over the last fifty years. Indeed, the difference between phonetically conditioned allophony and neutralisation, which involve only the phonetics and phonology, and cases where we also need to invoke morphological issues, is central to one of the most important current debates in phonology.

In the last chapter, generalisations about the distribution of allophones were stated in terms of rules, the assumption being that children learn these rules as they learn their native language, and start to see that forms fall into principled categories and behave according to regular patterns. Rule-based theories also include constraints – static, universal or language-specific statements of possibility in terms of segment shapes or combinations: these include both the redundancy rules discussed in Chapter 4, and phonotactic constraints. However, since the mid-1990s, an alternative approach has developed, as part of the phonological theory called Optimality Theory. Phonologists working in Optimality Theory do not write rules; they express *all* phonological generalisations using constraints. Instead of saying that a particular underlying or starting form changes into something else in a particular environment, which is what rules do, constraints set out what must happen, or what cannot happen, as in the examples in (6), which express regularities we have already identified for English.

(6) ASPIRATION: Voiceless stops are aspirated syllable-initially
    *s [b d g]   There are no sequences of [s] plus a voiced stop

In most versions of Optimality Theory, all the constraints are assumed to be universal and innate: children are born with the constraints already in place, so all they have to do is work out how important each constraint is in the structure of the language they are learning, and produce a ranking accordingly. For an English-learning child, the two constraints in (6) must be quite important, because it is true that voiceless stops *are* aspirated at the beginnings of syllables, and there *are* no sequences of [s] plus a voiced stop; consequently, English speakers will rank these two constraints high. However, for children learning a language *without* aspiration, or *with* clusters of [s] plus voiced stop, these constraints will not match the linguistic facts they hear; they will therefore be ranked low down in the list, so they have no obvious effect. On the other hand, a child learning German, say, would have to pay special attention to a constraint banning voiced stops from the ends of words, since this is a position of neutralisation in German, permitting only voiceless stops; but a child learning English will rank that constraint very low, as words like *hand, lob, fog* show that this constraint does not affect the structure of English.

Constraints of this sort seem to work quite well when we are dealing only with phonetic and phonological factors, and may be appropriate alternatives to rules in the clearly conditioned types of allophonic variation we have considered, and for neutralisation. However, they are not quite so helpful when it comes to the interaction of morphology and phonology, where alternations are often not clearly universally motivated, but involve facts about the structure and lexical items of that specific language alone. Analysing such cases using Optimality Theory may require a highly complex system of constraints, as we will have to accept that all the possible constraints for anything that could ever happen in any language are already there in every child's brain at birth. These issues are likely to lead to further debate in phonology in future years.

5.7 The phoneme system

The introduction of features reveals phonemes, not as the ultimate, smallest unit of the phonology, but as cover-symbols for a range of properties. However, it also permits a higher-level perspective, exploring natural classes, and the motivation for similar patterns of behaviour in groups of phonemes. These groupings can also be considered at the level of the phoneme system as a whole.

Just as the phoneme, although an abstract unit, seems to have some degree of reality for native speakers and to shape their perceptions, so the phoneme system, at an even higher level of abstraction, also reflects speakers' intuitions and may shape the development of a language.

For one thing, setting out a phoneme system can be extremely helpful to a phonologist in deciding which phonemes to propose for particular groups of allophones, and in checking that her decisions accord with native speakers' intuitions. For instance, some phonologists consider the English velar nasal as a phonemic sequence of /ng/ and /nk/, as it certainly was historically, even in cases where no [g] or [k] now appears phonetically: hence, *hang* would be analysed as /hang/, with the alveolar nasal having a velar allophone before velar plosives, and the velar plosive subsequently being deleted after a velar nasal at the ends of syllables. However, native speakers find the three nasals [m], [n] and [ŋ] easy to distinguish, although they may well not easily perceive cases which are more clearly allophones of /n/, such as the labiodental nasal [ɱ] in *unfortunate*. Their perception of /ŋ/ as separate from /n/ may be encouraged by the shape of the stop system in general, where voiced and voiceless plosives and a distinctive nasal stop go together at the labial /b p m/ and alveolar /d t n/ places of articulation, with /g k ŋ/ providing a parallel set of velars.

Similarly, consider the English affricates, [tʃ] and [dʒ], in *church* and *judge*. These could be phonemicised either as single units (albeit single units with two phases: recall that affricates have a stop phase, followed by a brief fricative phase as the stop is gradually released), or as clusters of consonants. In deciding which option to adopt, phonologists try to establish how the affricates behave. Do they follow the pattern of single phonemes in English, or do they act like clusters? In English, initial clusters of a plosive plus a fricative are extremely rare, and tend to be restricted to words obviously borrowed from other languages, like *psittacosis* or *dvandva* (a Sanskrit term for a type of compound word). However, the affricates occur quite freely both initially and finally (where such clusters are more common), making them seem less like clusters, and more like single units. Phonetically, affricates are also typically shorter than a sequence of stop plus fricative, so that in *why choose*, the fricative component in particular is significantly shorter than in *white shoes*. If the voiceless affricate were aspirated word-initially, or glottally reinforced word-finally, there would be additional good reasons for seeing this as essentially a stop, rather than a sequence.

Phoneme systems often seem to have the shape they do for essentially phonetic reasons. For instance, if there are too many distinctive sounds with similar features, they are likely to be misperceived, and may gradually merge historically: there is a general tendency for languages to have a reasonable margin of safety between sounds, so that words can be kept apart without the sort of effort which is inconsistent with fast, casual speech. Recall the discussion above of distinguishing <p> and <b> in writing, where there is a certain amount of tolerance built into the system concerning the placement of the loop; this would not be maintained if an intermediate symbol, <þ>, was introduced. Similarly, it is possible to keep the allophones of labial, alveolar and velar stops distinct, because there is a considerable amount of phonetic space between them in terms of articulation; in English, palatal allophones of /k g/, or dental allophones of /t d/ do not interfere with the realisations of any other stops. The story would be different if English also had contrastive palatal and dental stops.

As well as being determined by the need for reasonable margins of error, so that processes of assimilation, for instance, can take place without encroaching too greatly on the territory of adjacent phonemes, systems also seem to favour symmetry. Thus, English has pairs of contrastive voiced and voiceless stops at the labial, alveolar and velar places of articulation. If gaps arise in systems of this kind, they are very commonly filled by change in the language or by borrowing: the Old Irish stop system had a /b/ but no /p/, and /p/ was borrowed from Latin. In the case of the English fricatives, when voiced /v ð z/ came to contrast with pre-existing /f θ s/ in Middle English, there was no voiced counterpart for either /ʃ/ or /h/: however, /ʒ/ has subsequently been introduced by simplification of the [zj] cluster and in loans from French, while /h/ is increasingly marginal, appearing only syllable-initially; indeed, in some accents, like Cockney, it is routinely dropped in that position too, and might be said to be absent from the system altogether. Looking at phoneme systems may perhaps help phonologists identify weak spots in the language which are likely targets for later changes, as well as exemplifying some of the general principles native speakers pay attention to when learning and using their language.

Exercises

1. Find minimal pairs for the largest number of English consonant phonemes you can, in initial, medial and final positions in the word. Which list is longest? Note cases where you encounter defective distributions.

2. The 'liquid' consonants, namely /r/ and /l/, devoice in English after voiceless consonants, giving [pl̥eɪ] *play*, [tɹ̥eɪ] *tray*.

(a) Of the allophones [ɹ], [ɹ̥], [l] and [l̥], which are in complementary distribution?

(b) Which pairs of allophones would you assign to which phoneme, and how would you justify this decision?

(c) Write the allophonic rule determining the distribution of voiced and devoiced liquids.

3. Choose a nursery rhyme or short poem. Transcribe it (that is, write it out in IPA notation) as accurately as you can for your own accent, using V for vowels but giving as much detail on consonant allophones as you can.

4. In many (especially, but not only, urban) varieties of non-standard British English, the following pattern of distribution occurs for the voiceless plosives.

pill	[pʰɪl]	spill	[spɪl]	lip	[lɪʔ]
till	[tʰɪl]	still	[stɪl]	lit	[lɪʔ]
kill	[kʰɪl]	skill	[skɪl]	lick	[lɪʔ]

How can we describe the situation in word-final position phonologically? What symbol(s) might we choose to represent the unit(s) found here, and why? What would the most appropriate feature specification of the final unit of [lɪʔ] be?

Recommendations for reading

Difficulties with the phoneme, and issues of neutralisation and morphophonemics, are discussed in Giegerich (1992), Carr (1993), Durand (1990), Katamba (1988), Lass (1984) and Spencer (1996). Archangeli and Langendoen (1997) is the most accessible general introduction to Optimality Theory; Kager (1999) gives a more detailed account. Gussenhoven and Jacobs (1998) is a recent textbook on phonology written from an Optimality Theoretic point of view.

6 Describing vowels

6.1 Vowels versus consonants

Several examples in the last chapter involved vowels: for instance, we found that there is free variation for some speakers between [i] and [ɛ] in *economic*, but that these two vowels nonetheless contrast, as shown by minimal pairs like *pet* – *peat*, or *hell* – *heal*. We also saw that the usual contrast of /eɪ/, /ɛ/ and /æ/ is neutralised before /r/ for many General American speakers, who pronounce *Mary, merry* and *marry* homophonously. It follows that the central ideas of phonemic contrast, with minimal pairs determining the members of the phoneme system, and rules showing allophonic variation in different contexts, apply equally to vowels and to consonants; free variation, phonetic similarity and neutralisation affect both classes of sounds too. A more detailed demonstration of these issues for vowels, and the establishment of vowel phoneme systems for different varieties of English, will be the focus of Chapters 7 and 8.

However, when we turn to the physical description of actual vowel sounds, it is not possible simply to reuse the parameters and features already introduced for consonants. Of course, vowels and consonants are all speech sounds; and in English at least, they are all produced using the same pulmonic egressive airstream. In almost all other respects, however, the features which allow us to classify and understand consonants are less than helpful in distinguishing between vowels.

In Chapter 3, six articulatory parameters were introduced: knowing the value for each of these allowed us to describe English consonants unambiguously, and would extend to further consonants found in other languages. To describe a consonant in articulatory terms, we needed to know the airstream mechanism involved; the state of the glottis, determining whether the sound is voiced or voiceless; the position of the velum, which either allows or stops airflow through the nose, making the consonant nasal or oral; the manner of articulation, namely stop, affricate, fricative or approximant; whether airflow is central or lateral; and finally, the place of articulation, and consequently the identity and position of the active and passive articulators.

Unfortunately, almost none of these helps us in classifying vowels. All vowels, universally, are produced on a pulmonic egressive airstream, with central airflow: there is no contrast between central and lateral vowels. It is possible, but rare, for vowels to be voiceless or nasal; in English, however, all vowel phonemes are voiced and oral, and voiceless and nasal allophones appear only in very specific circumstances, as we shall see later. Vowels are all continuants: that is, airflow through the oral tract is not significantly obstructed during their production, so they are all approximants on the consonant manner classification: there are no stop, fricative or affricate vowels. Finally, although we shall distinguish between vowels in terms of place of articulation, the range of options is much more restricted than for consonants, where places from labial to glottal are distinguished in English alone. All vowels are produced in a very limited 'vowel space' in the centre of the oral tract, roughly between palatal and velar in consonantal terms; and the place of articulation will also be much more difficult to ascertain from self-observation, since the tongue never moves close enough to the roof of the mouth in vowel production to make its position easy to feel.

It follows that an adequate vowel classification requires new features and descriptive parameters which are better designed to capture the ways in which vowels *do* vary. This kind of situation, where two classes of objects or concepts share some essential unity, but need different descriptors, is not unique to vowels and consonants. For instance, plants and animals are both categories of living things; they both populate the world widely, and are mutually necessary in terms of their complementary roles in gas exchange, for instance. They both require the same basic nutrients, operate according to the same chemical principles, and have common structures, including identical cell types. However, there is just as little point in classifying plants according to whether or not they are mammals, or have feathers, or are carnivores or herbivores, as there is in categorising animals as being evergreen or dropping their leaves, bearing cones or flowers, or producing fruit or not. At that lower classificatory level, it is simply necessary to recognise the divergence of the two categories by using different distinguishing features. Equally, vowels and consonants are both speech sounds, and are both necessary for language, since they play complementary roles in structuring syllables and words. Both are formed by modifications of a moving airstream, carried out by the actions of the vocal folds and articulatory organs. However, below this very general, common level, consonants and vowels operate as different sets, and to allow us to produce as precise and insightful a classification of each set as possible, they must be described in different terms.

6.2 The anatomy of a vowel

In classifying vowels, we need not indicate airstream mechanism, since it will always be pulmonic egressive, and we can generally assume that vowels are all voiced and oral: allophonic exceptions will be discussed in Chapter 7. To describe vowels adequately and accurately, we then need to consider three different parameters, all of which can be seen as modifications of the place or manner of articulation continua for consonants: as we shall see, these are height, frontness and rounding. Additionally, vowels may be long or short (long ones are marked with a following ː below), and monophthongs or diphthongs. The examples in the sections below will be from Standard Southern British English (sometimes called RP, or Received Pronunciation), and General American, the most widely spoken variety of English in the United States, excluding the southern states, and the eastern seaboard, especially Boston, New England and New York City. SSBE and GA are generally thought of by English and American speakers respectively as not having any strong regional marking, and both are varieties highly likely to be heard in broadcasting, for instance in reading the television or radio news. Further accents will be introduced in Chapters 7 and 8.

6.2.1 The front–back dimension

Front vowels are produced with the front of the tongue raised towards the hard palate (although not raised enough, remember, to obstruct the airflow and cause local friction; vowels are approximants). The vowels in (1) are front. These could, in principle, equally be described as palatal, and this might be helpful in making phonological rules transparent: recall that in Chapter 4, the rule palatalising velar /k g/ before front vowels in *kitchen, key, give, geese* looked rather perplexing as the relationship between palatal and front was not obvious. However, calling front vowels palatal would be misleading, since frontness covers a larger area than [palatal], as we shall see below; and it contrasts with completely different alternatives, namely central and back, rather than labial, alveolar, dental, velar and so on.

(1) *Front vowels*

	SSBE	GA
kit	ɪ	ɪ
dress	ɛ	ɛ
trap	a	æ
fleece	iː	iː
face	eɪ	eɪ

Conversely, back vowels have the back of the tongue raised, towards the soft palate or velum. The vowels in (2) are back.

(2) *Back vowels*

	SSBE	GA
lot	ɒ	ɑː
foot	ʊ	ʊ
palm	ɑː	ɑː
thought	ɔː	ɔː
goat	oʊ	oː
goose	uː	uː

There is also a class of vowels between front and back: these are known as central vowels, and involve a raising of the body of the tongue towards the area where the hard and soft palate join. Central vowels are exemplified in (3). The most common of these in English, [ə], is known as schwa, and only appears in unstressed syllables.

(3) *Central vowels*

	SSBE	GA
<u>a</u>bout	ə	ə
nurse	ɜː	ɜr
strut	ʌ	ʌ

6.2.2 The high–low dimension

High vowels have the tongue raised most towards the roof of the mouth; if the raising was significantly greater, then friction would be produced, making a fricative consonant, not a vowel. The high vowels from the last section are in (4).

(4) *High vowels*

	SSBE	GA
kit	ɪ	ɪ
fleece	iː	iː
foot	ʊ	ʊ
goose	uː	uː

Low vowels are those where the tongue is not raised at all, but rather lowered from its resting position: when you produce a low vowel, you will be able to feel your mouth opening and your jaw dropping, even if it is not very easy to figure out quite what your tongue is doing. Low vowels are given in (5).

(5) *Low vowels*

	SSBE	GA
trap	a	æ
lot		ɑː
palm	ɑː	ɑː

Again, there is a further class intermediate between high and low, namely the mid vowels, shown in (6). These can if necessary be further subclassified as high mid (like the *face* and *goat* vowels) or low mid (like the *dress*, *thought*, *strut* vowels) depending on whether they are nearer the high end of the scale, or nearer the low end.

(6) *Mid vowels*

	SSBE	GA
face	eɪ	eɪ
goat	oʊ	oː
dress	ɛ	ɛ
lot	ɒ	
thought	ɔː	ɔː
about	ə	ə
nurse	ɜː	ɜr
strut	ʌ	ʌ

6.2.3 Lip position

In the high back [uː] vowel of *goose*, there is tongue raising in the region of the soft palate; but in addition, the lips are rounded. Vowels in any of the previous categories may be either rounded, where the lips are protruded forwards, or unrounded, where the lips may be either in a neutral position, or sometimes slightly spread (as for a high front vowel, like [iː] *fleece*). However, it is overwhelmingly more common cross-linguistically for back vowels to be rounded than for front ones, and for high vowels to be rounded than low ones; this is borne out in English, as you can see in (7).

(7) *Rounded vowels*

	SSBE	GA
lot	ɒ	
foot	ʊ	ʊ
thought	ɔː	ɔː
goat	oʊ	oː
goose	uː	uː

6.2.4 Length

Using these three dimensions of frontness, height and rounding, we can now define the vowel in *fleece* as high, front and unrounded; that in *goose* as high, back and rounded; and the unstressed vowel of *about*, schwa, as mid, central and unrounded. However, our elementary descriptions would class the *kit* vowel as high, front and unrounded, and the *foot* vowel as high, back and rounded; these labels make them indistinguishable from the clearly different vowels of *fleece* and *goose* respectively. SSBE and GA speakers very readily perceive the *fleece* and *kit* vowels, and the *goose* and *foot* vowels, as different; and there are plenty of minimal pairs to support a phoneme distinction, as in *peat – pit, leap – lip, Luke – look, fool – full*. This distinction is usually made in terms of vowel length: in SSBE and GA, the vowels in (8) are consistently produced as longer than those in (9).

(8) *Long vowels*

	SSBE	GA
fleece	iː	iː
goose	uː	uː
goat		oː
thought	ɔː	ɔː
palm	ɑː	ɑː
lot		ɑː
nurse	3ː	3r

(9) *Short vowels*

	SSBE	GA
kit	ɪ	ɪ
dress	ɛ	ɛ
trap	a	æ
lot	ɒ	
foot	ʊ	ʊ
about	ə	ə
strut	ʌ	ʌ

This is not to say, however, that the *only* difference between [iː] and [ɪ], or [uː] and [ʊ], is one of length: the quantity difference goes along with a difference in quality. [iː] is higher and fronter than [ɪ]; [uː] is higher and backer than [ʊ]; and similarly, [ɑː] in *palm* is lower and backer than the corresponding short [a] in *trap*. In general, long vowels in English are more peripheral, or articulated in a more extreme and definite way, than their short counterparts. Some phonologists use a feature [±tense] rather than length to express this difference, with the long, more peripheral vowels being [+tense], and the short, more centralised ones being [−tense], or lax.

6.2.5 Monophthongs and diphthongs

Most of the vowels we have considered so far have been monophthongs, in which the quality of the vowel stays fairly consistent from the beginning of its production to the end. However, there are also several diphthongs in English. Diphthongs change in quality during their production, and are typically transcribed with one starting point, and a quite different end point; as might be expected from this description, diphthongs are typically long vowels. In English, all diphthongs have the first element as longer and more prominent than the second, and are known as falling diphthongs. Three diphthongs are found very generally in accents of English, and are shown in (10).

(10) *Diphthongs (i)*

	SSBE	GA
price	aɪ	aɪ
mouth	aʊ	aʊ
choice	ɔɪ	ɔɪ

The long high-mid front and back vowels in *face* and *goat* are also characteristically diphthongal in SSBE and GA, as shown in (11).

(11) *Diphthongs (ii)*

	SSBE	GA
face	eɪ	eɪ
goat	oʊ	oː

Finally, SSBE has a third set of diphthongs, which are known as the centring diphthongs as they all have the mid central vowel schwa as the second element. These centring diphthongs developed historically before /r/, which was then lost following vowels in the ancestor of SSBE; they consequently appear mainly where there is an <r> in the spelling, although they have now been generalised to some other words, like *idea*.

GA speakers have a diphthong in *idea*, but still pronounce the historical [ɹ] in *near, square, force, cure* and therefore lack centring diphthongs in these words (see (12)).

(12) *Centring diphthongs*

	SSBE	GA
near	ɪə	ir
square	ɛə	ɛr
force	ɔə/ɔː	oːr
cure	ʊə	ʊr

6.3 Vowel classification

The labels outlined in the previous section are helpful, but may leave questions unresolved when used in comparisons between different languages or different accents of the same language. Thus, French [uː] in *rouge* is very close in quality to English [uː] in *goose*, but not identical; the French vowel is a little more peripheral, slightly higher and more back. Similarly, [oː] in *rose* for a GA speaker is slightly lower and more centralised than 'the same' vowel for a speaker of Scottish English. None of the descriptors introduced so far would allow us to make these distinctions clear, since in the systems of the languages or accents concerned, these pairs of vowels would quite appropriately be described as long, high, back and rounded, or long, high-mid, back and rounded respectively.

Furthermore, a classification of this sort, based essentially on articulation, is arguably less appropriate for vowels than for consonants. In uttering a vowel, the important thing is to produce a particular sort of auditory impression, so that someone listening understands which vowel in the system you are aiming at; but it does not especially matter which articulatory strategies you use to convey that auditory impression. If you were asked to produce an [uː], but not allowed to round your lips, then with a certain amount of practice you could make at least something very similar; and yet it would not be a rounded vowel in the articulatory sense, although you would have modified the shape of your vocal tract to make it sound like one. This is not possible with most consonants, where the auditory impression depends on the particular articulators used, and how close they get, not just the overall shape of the vocal tract and the effect that has on a passing airstream. It is true that the whole oral tract is a continuum, but it is easier to see the places for consonants as definite 'stopping off places' along that continuum, helped by the fact that most consonants are obstruents, and we can feel what articulators are involved.

One possible solution is to abandon an articulatory approach to vowel classification altogether, and turn instead to an analysis of the speech wave itself: but acoustic phonetics is beyond the scope of this book. In any case, it is true that most speakers of particular accents or even languages will produce certain vowels in an articulatorily similar fashion. For comparative purposes, what we need is an approach which allows vowel qualities to be expressed as relative rather than absolute values.

We can achieve this comparative perspective by plotting vowels on a diagram rather than simply defining them in isolation. The diagram conventionally used for this purpose is known as the Vowel Quadrilateral, and is an idealised representation of the vowel space, roughly between palatal and velar, where vowels can be produced in the vocal tract. The left edge corresponds to the palatal area, and hence to front vowels, and the right edge to the velar area, and back vowels. The top line extends slightly further than the bottom one because there is physically more space along the roof of the mouth than along the base. Finally, the chart is conventionally divided into six sectors, allowing high, high-mid, low-mid and low vowels to be plotted, as well as front, central and back ones. There is no way of reading information on rounding directly from the vowel quadrilateral, so that vowels are typically plotted using an IPA symbol rather than a dot; it is essential to learn these IPA symbols to see which refer to rounded, and which to unrounded vowels. The SSBE and GA monophthongs discussed in Section 6.2 are plotted in (13); the monophthongs of the two accents are similar enough to include on a single chart, although the [ɒ] vowel is bracketed, since it occurs in SSBE but not in GA, where words like *lot* have low [ɑː] instead.

(13) *SSBE and GA monophthongs*

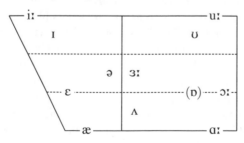

Diphthongs are not really well suited to description in terms of the labels introduced above, since they are essentially trajectories of articulation starting at one point and moving to another; in this respect, they are parallel to affricate consonants. Saying that [ɔɪ] in *noise*, for instance, is a low-mid back rounded vowel followed by a high front unrounded vowel would not distinguish it from a sequence of vowels in different syllables or even different words; but the diphthong in *noise* is clearly different from the sequence of independent vowels in *law is*. Using the vowel quadrilateral, we can plot the changes in pronunciation involved in the production of a diphthong using arrows, as in (14). Plotting several diphthongs in this way can lead to a very messy chart, but it is nonetheless helpful in clarifying exactly how a particular diphthong is composed, and what its starting and stopping points are; and the notation reminds us that a symbolic representation like [ɔɪ] is actually short-hand for a gradual articulatory and auditory movement.

(14)

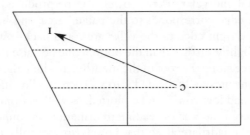

However, plotting vowels on the quadrilateral is only reliable if the person doing the plotting is quite confident about the quality she is hearing, and this can be difficult to judge without a good deal of experience, especially if a non-native accent or language is being described. To provide a universal frame of reference for such situations, phoneticians often work with an idealised set of vowels known as the Cardinal Vowels. For our purposes, we need introduce only the primary cardinals, which are conventionally numbered 1–8. Cardinal Vowel 1 is produced by raising and fronting the tongue as much as possible; any further, and a palatal fricative would result. This vowel is like a very extreme form of English [iː] in *fleece*. Its opposite, in a sense, is Cardinal Vowel 5, the lowest, backest vowel that can be produced without turning into a fricative; this is like a lower, backer version of SSBE [ɑː] in *palm*. Between these two fixed points, organised equidistantly around the very edges of the vowel quadrilateral, are the other six primary cardinal vowels, as shown in (15). Cardinal 8 is like English [uː] in *goose*, but again higher and backer; similarly, Cardinals 3, 4 and 6 can be compared with the vowels of English *dress*, *trap* and *thought*, albeit more extreme in articulation. Finally, Cardinals 2 and 7 are, as we shall see in Chapters 7 and 8, like the monophthongal pronunciations of a Scottish English speaker in words like *day*, *go*. The steps between Cardinals 1–4 and 5–8 should be articulatorily and acoustically equidistant, and lip rounding also increases from Cardinals 6, through 7, to 8.

(15) *The Primary Cardinal Vowels*

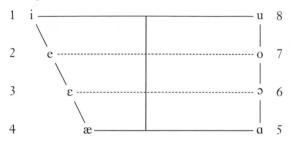

In truth, the only way of learning the Cardinal Vowels properly, and ensuring that they can act as a fixed set of reference points as they were designed to do, is to learn them from someone who already knows the system, and do a considerable amount of practice (various tapes and videos are available if you wish to do this). For the moment, what matters is to have an idea of what the Cardinal Vowels are, and what the theoretical justification for such a system is, in terms of describing the vowels of an unfamiliar language, or giving a principled account of the differences between the vowels of English and some other language, or different accents of English. We turn to such differences, as well as a more detailed outline of English vowel phonemes and allophones, in the next two chapters.

Exercises

1. (a) Which of the following words contains a rounded vowel?
        put   seek   hook   grew   grey   hoe   hold
    (b) Which of the following words contains a front vowel?
        see   seat   met   tap   throw   tape   through
    (c) Which of the following words contains a high vowel?
        see   seat   steak   throw   list   lost   through
    (d) Which of the following words contains a central vowel?
        about   put   luck   hit   purse   father   kept
    (e) Which of the following words contains a high back vowel?
        put   love   hit   heat   luck   look   food

2. (a) What do the vowels in these words have in common?
        bet   hair   rose   post   love   purse   mate
    (b) What do the vowels in these words have in common?
        see   leap   weird   pit   fiend   miss   crypt

    (c) What do the vowels in these words have in common?
        height   boy   try   noise   loud   crowd   fine
    (d) What do the vowels in these words have in common?
        flea   rude   piece   flu   stew   leave   sees

3. Make vowel quadrilateral diagrams for all the diphthongs of SSBE, showing the position of the first and second elements and drawing lines and arrows connecting them.

4. Give as detailed a description as you can of the vowels in the following words:

    father leaving hear thoroughly fast haste lookalike sausage ooze

Recommendations for reading

The reading recommended in Chapter 3 is equally suitable for this chapter, although you will wish to concentrate this time on sections relating to vowels rather than consonants. Sound changes, and their contribution to the present-day structure of the language, have been mentioned several times above and in earlier chapters: if you are interested in language change, you might like to consult Campbell (1998) or Trask (1996).

7 Vowel phonemes

7.1 The same but different again

As we saw in the last chapter, most of the features which work well in classifying and describing consonants are entirely inappropriate for vowels, while vowels vary in dimensions (such as tongue height) which are not relevant for consonants. However, when we turn to the criteria for establishing phonemes, and the exceptions to these reviewed in Chapters 2 and 5, it turns out that vowels and consonants behave very similarly indeed. The sections below therefore fulfil a dual role of providing more information about vowels, while allowing some revision of notions like complementary distribution, allophonic rules, free variation, neutralisation and phonetic similarity, which were first introduced mainly in connection with consonants.

7.2 Establishing vowel contrasts

7.2.1 Minimal pairs

Minimal pairs and the commutation test are the main tools available to the phonologist in ascertaining phonemic contrast among both consonants and vowels. A minimal pair list for SSBE vowels appears in (1).

(1) *Vowel minimal pairs*

bit	/ɪ/
bet	/ɛ/
bat	/æ/
but	/ʌ/
beat	/iː/
bait	/eɪ/
Bart	/ɑː/
boat	/oʊ/
bought	/ɔː/

boot	/uː/
bite	/aɪ/
bout	/aʊ/
sherb<u>e</u>t	/ə/
Bert	/ɜː/

The list above provides evidence for almost all phonemically con-trastive vowels of SSBE, with a very small number of exceptions. Since schwa only appears in unstressed syllables, where most of the other vowels cannot appear, we must make do with near-minimal comparisons in this case, contrasting the second, unstressed syllable of *sherbet* with the various stressed syllables in (1). The short vowels /ʊ/ and /ɒ/, and the centring diphthongs, which were listed as SSBE vowels in the last chap-ter, do not appear in the selected context /b-t/; but the additional data in (2) shows that /ʊ/ and /ɒ/ on the one hand, and the three centring diphthongs on the other, contrast both with one another and with rep-resentative members of the list in (1). Phonemic contrast is a transitive relationship, meaning that if phoneme *a* contrasts with phoneme *b*, and phoneme *b* contrasts with phoneme *c*, then phonemes *a* and *c* also contrast: this means that if a contrast can be established between one of the 'left-out' vowels and any vowel in (1), then that vowel can be taken as contrasting with all the vowels in (1).

(2) pit /ɪ/   put /ʊ/   pot /ɒ/   peat /iː/   etc.
     leer /ɪə/   lair /ɛə/   lure /ʊə/   lore /ɔː/

Sets of minimal pairs like this may work very well for one accent, but not for another. Some disparities of this sort were discussed in earlier chapters; for instance, minimal pairs like *lock* /k/ versus *loch* /x/, or *witch* /w/ versus *which* /ʍ/ will be relevant for many Scottish speakers in establishing the voiceless velar and labial-velar fricative phonemes, but both members of the pairs will have /k/ and /w/ respectively in many other accents of English. Although this was a rather minor issue for consonants, it is much more important in discussing vowel phoneme systems, since as we shall see in Chapter 8, most accent variation in English involves vowels.

7.2.2 Standard lexical sets

The oppositions established for SSBE in (1) and (2) cannot, then, be transferred automatically to other accents. For instance, General American has no centring diphthong phonemes; *leer*, *lair* and *lure* have the /iː/, /eɪ/ and /uː/ vowels of *beat*, *bait* and *boot*, followed in each case by /r/. GA also lacks the /ɒ/ vowel of SSBE *pot*; but we cannot assume that all the words with /ɒ/ in SSBE have a single, different phoneme in GA. On the contrary, some words, like *lot, pot, sock, possible* have GA /ɑː/ (as also in *palm, father, Bart, far* in both accents); but others, including *cloth, cough, cross, long* have GA /ɔː/ (as also in *thought, sauce, north, war* in both accents).

It follows that lists of minimal pairs are suitable when our goal is the establishment of a phoneme system for a single accent; but they may not be the best option when different accents are being compared. An alternative is to use a system introduced by John Wells (see Recommendations for reading), involving 'standard lexical sets', as shown in (3). The key word for each standard lexical set appears conventionally in capital letters, and is shorthand for a whole list of other words sharing the same vowel, although the precise vowel they do share may vary from accent to accent.

(3) *Standard Lexical Sets*

SSBE	GA	Set number	Keyword
ɪ	ɪ	1	KIT
ɛ	ɛ	2	DRESS
a	æ	3	TRAP
ɒ	ɑː	4	LOT
ʌ	ʌ	5	STRUT
ʊ	ʊ	6	FOOT
ɑː	æ	7	BATH
ɒ	ɔː	8	CLOTH
ɜː	ɜ	9	NURSE
iː	iː	10	FLEECE
eɪ	eɪ	11	FACE
ɑː	ɑː	12	PALM
ɔː	ɔː	13	THOUGHT
oʊ	oː	14	GOAT
uː	uː	15	GOOSE
aɪ	aɪ	16	PRICE
ɔɪ	ɔɪ	17	CHOICE
aʊ	aʊ	18	MOUTH
ɪə	ir	19	NEAR
ɛə	eɪr	20	SQUARE
ɑː	ɑr	21	START
ɔː	ɔr	22	NORTH
ɔː	or	23	FORCE
ʊə	ur	24	CURE

ɪ	i	25	HAPPY
ə	ər	26	LETTER
ə	ə	27	COMMA

These lexical sets allow comparison between accents to be made much more straightforwardly: we can now ask which vowel speakers of a particular accent have in the KIT set, or whether they have the same vowel in NORTH and FORCE (as SSBE does) or two different vowels (as GA does). We could add that many speakers of Northern English will have /ʊ/ in STRUT as well as FOOT, and /a/ in BATH as well as TRAP, pinpointing two of the differences most commonly noted between north and south. The point of the standard lexical sets is not to show that oppositions exist in all these contexts: in fact, there may be no accent of English which contrasts twenty-seven phonemically different vowels in the twenty-seven lexical sets (or even twenty-four, for the stressed vowels). Instead, the aim is to allow differences between accents (and sometimes between speakers of the same accent, perhaps in different generations) to be pinpointed and discussed.

More detail on accent variation will be given in the next chapter. For the moment, to illustrate the usefulness of the standard lexical sets, the vowels of two further accents are given in (4). Standard Scottish English (or SSE) is the Scottish equivalent of SSBE: a relatively unlocalised, socially prestigious accent. Many middle-class Scots have SSE as a native variety; many others use it in formal situations, and it is widely heard in the media, in education and in the Scottish Parliament. It is to be contrasted with Scots, sometimes called 'broad Scots', a divergent range of non-standard Scottish dialects which differ from English Standard English not only in phonetics and phonology, but also in vocabulary and grammar. The final example is New Zealand English, a relatively recent variety which shares some characteristics with the other extraterritorial Englishes spoken in Australia and South Africa, but also has some distinctive characteristics of its own, notably the fact that schwa appears in stressed position, in the KIT lexical set.

(4) SSE	NZE	Set number	Keyword
ɪ	ə	1	KIT
ɛ	e	2	DRESS
a	ɛ	3	TRAP
ɒ	ɒ	4	LOT
ʌ	ʌ	5	STRUT
u	ʊ	6	FOOT
a	aː	7	BATH
ɒ	ɒ	8	CLOTH

ʌr	ɜː	9	NURSE
i	iː	10	FLEECE
e	ɛɪ	11	FACE
a	aː	12	PALM
ɒ	ɔː	13	THOUGHT
o	əu	14	GOAT
u	ʉː	15	GOOSE
ʌɪ	aɪ	16	PRICE
ɔɪ	ɔɪ	17	CHOICE
ʌʊ	aʊ	18	MOUTH
ir	iə	19	NEAR
er	eə	20	SQUARE
ar	aː	21	START
ɒr	ɔː	22	NORTH
or	ɔː	23	FORCE
ur	uə	24	CURE
i	i	25	HAPPY
ər	ə	26	LETTER
ʌ	ə	27	COMMA

A number of differences between these accents, and between each of them and SSBE or GA, can be read off these lists. For instance, SSE does not contrast the TRAP and PALM vowels, so that *Sam* and *psalm*, which are minimal pairs for all the other varieties considered so far, are homophonous for Scottish speakers, both having short low front /a/. In NZE, *Sam* and *psalm* do form a minimal pair, but not with low short front /a/ or /æ/ versus low long back /ɑː/: instead, in NZE we find mid short front /ɛ/ as opposed to low long back front /aː/. Both the TRAP and DRESS vowels in NZE are higher than those of SSBE or GA, while the long vowels of FLEECE, FACE, GOAT and GOOSE are very characteristically diphthongs.

Recall, however, that phonemes are abstract units, and thus could potentially be symbolised using any IPA, or indeed any other character. The symbols chosen for particular phonemes in the lists above are not the only possibilities; they reflect a choice made by a particular phonologist. I have elected to use a symbol for each phoneme, in each accent, which corresponds to one of the main allophones of that phoneme: that is, in many cases speakers of the accent in question will actually pronounce the symbol given in the list, with its normal IPA value. Thus, NZE speakers will often say [ɛ] in *trap*, and [e] in *dress*, and will typically have a diphthongal pronunciation of *fleece, goose, goat* and *face*. However, for some phonologists the symbols used in (4) would not be the most obvious choices. This highlights a decision phonologists must make in establishing a phoneme system. On the one hand, we may wish our phonemes to be fairly concrete, reflecting quite closely what speakers actually do in at least some of their everyday pronunciations; this is the choice made here. It follows that there will be significant symbol differences between the vowel systems of different accents. On the other hand, some phonologists feel it is more important to reflect the fact that English is a single language, and believe that speakers must have common mental representations to allow them to understand one another, even if they speak rather different accents. In that case, common phoneme symbols might be chosen. For instance, instead of using /ɪi/ for FLEECE in NZE, we would select /iː/, stressing that this is the same phoneme as in SSBE or GA, although there would then have to be an allophonic rule to say that this phoneme is very typically diphthongised for most New Zealanders.

The second solution has the advantage that it stresses the common features speakers of English might share, at least in terms of mental representations, although they may sound very different in actual conversation. It therefore maintains a strong difference between abstract phonology, and concrete phonetics: the /a/ phoneme in TRAP would be low [a] for SSBE, but low mid [ɛ] for NZE, while the /ɛ/ phoneme of DRESS would be high mid [e] for NZE, and low mid [ɛ] in all the other accents we have examined, meaning that phonemes potentially have very different realisations, and the same realisation can belong to different phonemes in different accents. At this point, we do not know enough about how speakers store and process their language mentally to prove which is the most appropriate solution; but it is worth asking how speakers would learn a very abstract system, which does not reflect the phonetic qualities they hear around them during language acquisition. If a New Zealander pronounces the FLEECE vowel as a diphthong, and hears NZE or Australian English (which also tends to have a diphthong here) much more often than British or American accents, why would such a speaker assume this vowel phoneme should be stored as anything other than a diphthong? And why should the 'right' value for the phoneme corresponds to what is pronounced in British or American English, rather than in New Zealand or Australia? The decision between representations which are close to phonetic reality, but with considerable accent variation and potentially rather messy systems, or rather abstract phonemes, with streamlined and economical systems unifying the speakers of different varieties, must be confronted whenever we move away from surface phonetics and into phonology. In this book, I shall continue to use phoneme symbols which correspond to major allophones of those phonemes in the accent concerned; but other, more abstract alternatives can be found in the recommended further reading.

7.3 Vowel features and allophonic rules

Once phonemic contrasts have been established for the accent in question, and the appropriate representation for each phoneme has been selected, the realisations of those phonemes must be determined and rules written to describe allophonic variation. Again, features and rule notation can be used to formalise these statements. We saw in Chapter 4 that vowels are [+syllabic, −consonantal, +sonorant, +voice, −nasal]. To distinguish English vowels appropriately, we also require the features [±high], [±mid] for the dimension of tongue height; [±front], [±back] for place of articulation; and [±round]. These give the illustrative matrix in (5).

(5)	[high]	[mid]	[front]	[back]	[round]
[i]	+	−	+	−	−
[e]	+	+	+	−	−
[ɛ]		+	+		
[a]	−	−	+	−	−
[u]	+	−	−	+	+
[o]	+	+	−	+	+
[ɔ]	−	+	−	+	+
[ɑ]	−	−	−	+	−
[ə]	−	+	−	−	−

These features can distinguish four contrastive degrees of vowel height, and three degrees of frontness, which allows all varieties of English to be described. However, /iː/ and /ɪ/, and /uː/ and /ʊ/, will be identical in this matrix. In SSBE and GA, the former in each pair is typically long, and the latter short; and long vowels are also articulated more extremely, or more peripherally than corresponding short ones: the long high front vowel is higher and fronter than the short high front vowel, while the long high back vowel is higher and backer than its short counterpart. The question is whether we regard this as primarily a quality or a quantity difference. If we take quality as primary, we can regard /i/, /u/, /ɑ/, /ɔ/ as [+tense], or more peripheral, and simply write a redundancy rule to say that all tense vowels are phonetically long. On the other hand, we could do the opposite, and take length as the important factor, so these vowels are long /iː/, /uː/, /ɑː/ and /ɔː/, and redundantly also more peripheral.

For most accents of English, we could choose either solution, although most phonologists would select either length or tenseness as relevant at the phoneme level, with the other simply following automatically, to minimise redundancy in the system. However, in SSE and Scots dialects, it matters which we choose. This is because vowels in Scottish accents (and some related Northern Irish accents) are unique among varieties of English in one respect: we can predict where vowels are phonetically long, and where they are phonetically short. Vowels become long before /r v ð z ʒ/ and at the end of a word, but they are short everywhere else, as shown in (6).

(6) *The Scottish Vowel Length Rule*

/i/	[i]	beat	wreath	leaf	bean
	[iː]	beer	wreathe	leave	agree
/o/	[o]	boat	close (Adj)	foal	ode
	[oː]	bow	close (V)	four	owe

/ɪ/, /ɛ/ and /ʌ/, which are short and lax in other accents, do not lengthen in any circumstances. In SSE and Scots, then, we can define the two classes of phonemic vowels as lax (the three which never lengthen) and tense (the others, which are sometimes long and sometimes short, in predictably different environments). It is possible to predict length from [±tense], but not the other way around. The allophonic rule involved will then state that tense vowels lengthen before /r/, before a voiced fricative, or before a word boundary (that is, in word-final position), to account for the data in (6).

Other allophonic rules are more general. For instance, in all varieties of English, vowels become nasalised immediately before nasal consonants; the velum lowers in anticipation of the forthcoming nasal, and allows air to flow through the nasal as well as the oral cavity during the production of the vowel. If you produce *cat* and *can*, then regardless of whether your vowel is front or back, there will be a slight difference in quality due to nasalisation in the second case; you may hear this as a slight lowering of the pitch. This rule is shown in (7); note that the symbol V here means 'any vowel'.

(7)   V   →   [+nasal]   / _____ [+nasal]

Just as for consonants, then, some allophonic rules specifying the realisations of vowel phonemes are found very generally in English (and may in fact, as in the case of the nasalisation process in (7), reflect universal phonetic tendencies); others, like the Scottish Vowel Length Rule, are peculiar to certain accents.

7.4 Phonetic similarity and defective distribution

Just as we saw for consonants in Chapter 5, phonetic similarity can help us decide which vowel allophones to assign to which phonemes, and defective distributions hinder our decision-making. For instance, schwa in accents other than NZE is confined to unstressed positions, and therefore does not strictly speaking contrast with most other vowels. Its defective distribution means it could be regarded as the unstressed allophone of almost any other vowel phoneme. So, schwa appears in the unstressed syllables of *about, father, fathom, sherbet, pompous*; but which vowel phoneme is involved in each case? Since speakers do not tend to produce vowels other than schwa in any of these forms, even when speaking rather carefully, it is difficult to say. We could say that there is wholesale neutralisation of vowel phonemes in unstressed syllables; alternatively, because speakers of English can hear the difference between schwa and other vowels quite reliably, and seem to regard schwa as a distinct vowel, the best solution might be to accept that schwa is a phoneme of English in its own right, albeit with a defective distribution.

Again as with consonants, defective distributions often result from language change. For instance, spelling evidence from Old English in-dicates that a much wider range of vowels was probably found in unstressed syllables at that period; these have gradually merged into schwa during the history of English. Similarly, the centring diphthongs of SSBE are generally found where there is an <r> in the spelling, and where other accents, like SSE and GA, have combinations of a vowel found elsewhere in the system, plus [ɹ]. Historically, all varieties of English followed the SSE/GA pattern; but accents like SSBE lost [ɹ] in certain contexts, with a related change in the realisation of vowels producing the centring diphthongs.

As for phonetic similarity, it will again help to resolve situations where one allophone could potentially belong to more than one phoneme, although phonologists (and native speakers) apply this criterion so auto-matically as to scarcely justify making it an explicit step in phonemic analysis. In the case of vowel nasalisation before nasals, for instance, there is a situation of complementary distribution between ALL nasal-ised allophones on the one hand, since these can appear only adjacent to a nasal consonant, and ALL oral allophones on the other. It is theor-etically possible that [uː] and [ĩː], or [ɛ] and [õ], might be assigned to the same phoneme, if we took only complementary distribution into account. However, since the members of these vowel pairs differ from one another with respect to more features than simply [nasal], notably in terms of frontness; and since there are alternative pairings available, namely [iː] and [ĩː], or [ʊ] and [ũ], where nasalisation is the only difference at issue, these minimally different, more phonetically similar pairings will be used in establishing which two realisations belong to each phoneme.

7.5 Free variation, neutralisation and morphophonemics

Some examples involving free variation between vowel phonemes were reviewed in Chapter 5: for instance, *economic* can be pronounced, for the same speaker, with the DRESS vowel on some occasions and the FLEECE vowel on others, and although this conflicts with the requirement that different phonemes should not be substitutable without causing a change in meaning to be conveyed, such a marginal case involving only a single lexical item should not in fact compromise the distinction between /ɛ/ and /iː/, given the significant number of minimal pairs establishing their contrast.

Free variation also occurs between allophones of a single phoneme. This again correlates with sociolinguistic rather than linguistic conditioning. For instance, in NZE some speakers produce /ɜː/, the NURSE vowel, with lip-rounding, more significantly so in informal circumstances. Similarly, New Yorkers may produce the FLEECE and GOOSE vowels as monophthongs in formal situations, but prefer diphthongs in casual speech; and the quality of the diphthongs varies too, with [ii], [uu] being more common for middle-class speakers, but more central first elements, and hence a greater distance between the two parts of the diphthongs, for working-class speakers. Some cases of free variation reflect language change in progress: so, in SSBE older speakers may still produce centring diphthongs in CURE and SQUARE words, while younger ones almost invariably smoothe these diphthongs out and produce monopthongal [ɔː], [ɛː]. Younger speakers might use the pronunciations more typical of the older generation when they are talking to older relatives, or in formal circumstances.

Cases of neutralisation tend not to be subject to sociolinguistic influence in this way, but rather reflect a tendency for certain otherwise contrastive sets or pairs of vowels to fall together with a single realisation in a particular phonological context. In the last chapter, we saw that the DRESS, TRAP and SQUARE vowels are neutralised for many GA speakers before /r/, so that *merry*, *marry* and *Mary* become homophonous: in this context, rather than the usual /ɛ/, /æ/, /eɪ/ opposition, we might propose archiphonemic /E/, realised as [ɛ]. Neutralisations of this sort are extremely common for English vowels. To take just two further examples, speakers from the southern states of the USA have a neutralisation of the KIT and DRESS vowels before /n/, so that *pin* and *pen* are homophonous; and for many speakers of SSE and Scots, the opposition between the KIT and STRUT vowels is suspended before /r/, so that *fir* and *fur* are both pronounced with [ʌ].

However, whereas suspension of contrast takes place in a particular phonological context, and will affect all lexical items with that context, in other cases we are dealing with an interaction of morphology and phonology; here, we cannot invoke neutralisation. For instance, the discussion of the Scottish Vowel Length Rule above does not quite tell the full story, since we also find alternations of long and short vowels in the cases in (8).

(8) *Short*   *Long*
    greed   agreed
    brood   brewed
    bonus   slowness
    typing   tie-pin

From the Scottish Vowel Length Rule examples considered earlier, we concluded that vowel length is not contrastive in SSE and Scots, since it was possible to predict that long vowels appear before certain consonants or at the end of a word, while short ones appear elsewhere. However, the data in (8) appear, on purely phonological grounds, to constitute minimal pairs for short and long vowels. In fact, what seems to matter is the structure of the words concerned. The vowels in the 'Long' column of (8) are in a sense word-final; they precede the inflectional ending [d] marking past tense; or the suffix *-ness*; or appear at the end of the first element of a compound, which is a word in its own right, as in *tie*. This is not true for the 'Short' column, where the words are not separable in this way. The Scottish Vowel Length Rule must therefore be rewritten to take account of the morphological structure of words: it operates before /r/ and voiced fricatives, at the end of a word, and also at the end of a morpheme, or meaningful unit within the word; in the cases in (8), the affected vowel is at the end of a stem.

In other cases, different vowel phonemes alternate with one another before particular suffixes, as we found for consonants in Chapter 5 where the final [k] of *electric* became [s] or [ʃ] before certain suffixes, as in *electricity* and *electrician*. One of the best-known cases in English, and one which affects all varieties, involves pairs of words like those in (9).

(9) divine – divinity   line – linear   /aɪ/ – /ɪ/
     serene – serenity   supreme – supremacy   /iː/ – /ɛ/
     sane – sanity   explain – explanatory   /eɪ/ – /æ/

These Vowel Shift alternations (so-called because the patterns reflect the operation of a sound change called the Great Vowel Shift several hundred years ago) involve pairs of phonemes which very clearly contrast in English – the members of the PRICE and KIT, FLEECE and DRESS, and FACE and TRAP pairs of standard lexical sets. Minimal pairs are common for all of these (take *type* and *tip*, *peat* and *pet*, *lake* and *lack*, for instance). However, the presence of each member of these pairs can be predicted in certain contexts only; and native speakers tend to regard the pairs involved, such as *divine* and *divinity*, as related forms of the same word. This is not neutralisation, because the context involved is not specifically phonetic or phonological: it is morphological. That is, what matters is not the length of the word, or the segment following the vowel in question, but the presence or absence of one of a particular set of suffixes. In underived forms (that is, those with no suffix at all) we find the tense or long vowel, here /aɪ/, /iː/ or /eɪ/; but in derived forms, with a suffix like *-ity*, *-ar*, *-acy*, *-ation*, a corresponding lax or short vowel /ɪ/, /ɛ/ or /æ/ appears instead. This alternation is a property of the lexical item concerned; vowel changes typically appear when certain suffixes are added, but there are exceptions like *obese*, with /iː/ in the underived stem, and the same vowel (rather than the /ɛ/ we might predict) in *obesity*, regardless of the presence of the suffix *-ity*. Opting out in this way does not seem to be a possibility in cases of neutralisation, but is quite common in cases of morphophonemics, or the interaction between phonology and morphology.

To put it another way, not all alternations involving morphology are completely productive. Some are: this means that every single relevant word of English obeys the regularity involved (so, all those nouns which form their plural using a *-s* suffix will have this pronounced as [s] after a voiceless final sound in the stem, [z] after a voiced one, and [ɪz] after a sibilant; not only this, but any new nouns which are borrowed into English from other languages, or just made up, will also follow this pattern). Others are fairly regular, but not entirely so: this goes for the Vowel Shift cases above. And yet others are not regular at all, but are simply properties of individual lexical items which children or second-language learners have to learn as such. The fact that *teach* has the past tense *taught* is an idiosyncrasy of modern English which has to be mastered; but although knowing this relationship will help a learner of English to use *teach* and *taught* appropriately, it will not help when it comes to learning other verbs, because *preach* does not have the past tense **praught*, and *caught* does not have the present tense **ceach*. Knowing where we should draw the line between extremely regular cases which clearly involve exceptionless rules or generalisations, fairly regular ones which may be stated as rules with exceptions, and one-off (or several-off) cases where there is no rule at all but a good deal of rote-learning, is one of the major challenges of morphophonology. The only comfort is that native speakers, at least during acquisition and sometimes later too, find it just as much of a challenge, as amply demonstrated by overgeneralisations like past-tense *swang* from *swing* (on the pattern of *swim* – *swam*) or past-tense [trɛt] from *treat* (on the pattern of *meet* – *met*).

Exercises

1. Make phonemic transcriptions for the following words, for (a) SSBE, (b) GA, (c) SSE and (d) NZE.
   water grass righteousness holiday pilchard following northeast spoonful

2. Write rules for the following processes:
   (a) Front rounded vowels become unrounded before velars
   (b) Vowels devoice before voiceless consonants
   (c) /iː uː ɪ ʊ/ become /eː oː ɛ ɒ/ after clusters of two consonants, the second of which is a nasal
   (d) /ɑː ɔː/ become /uː/ before palatal consonants or at the beginnings of words

3. Go back to the nursery rhyme or short poem you transcribed in the exercises to Chapter 5. Now, instead of using V for all vowels, transcribe the vowels using the reference accent (from SSBE, GA, SSE and NZE) with which you are most familiar, or which is closest to your own.

4. Make a list of the standard lexical sets, and write down which vowel phoneme you have in each of the twenty-seven cases. Which vowel symbols have you chosen to symbolise each phoneme, and why?

Recommendations for reading

The general phonology textbooks recommended for Chapter 5 are also relevant here. The standard lexical set approach is set out in detail in Wells (1983), which also provides a wealth of information on varieties of English. More detail on the linguistic situation in Scotland and the varieties spoken there can be found in Jones (1997).

8 Variation between accents

8.1 The importance of accent

Every speaker of English has a particular system of his or her own, known by linguists as that individual's idiolect. However, considering language only at the idiolectal level might produce extremely thorough and detailed descriptions, but would give rather little insight into why individuals speak in the way they do. To understand this, we must identify higher-level groupings, and investigate geographical and social accents. That is to say, individuals adopt a particular mode of speech (or more accurately, move along a continuum of modes of speech) depending on who they want to identify with, who they are talking to, and what impression they want to make. Not all these 'decisions' are conscious, of course. Small children learn to speak as their immediate family members do; but quite soon, the peer group at school (even nursery) becomes at least equally important; and later, older children, then television presenters, actors or sporting heroes may become role models, leading to modifications in accent. Consequently, age-related differences appear in all varieties; some will be transient, as a particular TV show falls out of fashion and the words or pronunciations borrowed from it disappear; others will become entrenched in young people's language, and may persist into adulthood, becoming entirely standard forms for the next generation.

This flexibility, and the associated facts of variation and gradual change, mean that phonologists face a Catch-22 situation. On the one hand, describing idiolects will give seriously limited information, since it will not reveal the groups an individual belongs to, or the dynamics of those groups. On the other hand, we must take care that the groups are not described at too abstract a level. Any description of 'an accent' is necessarily an idealisation, since no two speakers will use precisely the same system in precisely the same way: our physical idiosyncrasies, different backgrounds, and different preferences and aspirations will see to that. Nonetheless, two speakers of, say, Scottish Standard English, or New Zealand English, will have a common core of features, which allows them to be grouped together by speakers of the same accent, by speakers of other accents, and by phonologists. Not everyone is equally adept at making these identifications, of course. Speakers of other varieties may succeed in placing accents only within a very wide geographical boundary: thus, a speaker of GA may have difficulty in distinguishing a Scottish from an Irish speaker, while conversely, a Scot may confuse Americans and Canadians. Within groups, however, much more subtle distinctions are perceived and have geographical or social meaning: hence, one speaker of SSE may identify another as coming from Glasgow rather than Edinburgh, and perhaps even from a particular area of the city; and may well base assumptions to do with social class and level of education on those linguistic factors.

Accent is clearly extremely important, as one of the major tools we use in drawing inferences about our fellow humans, and in projecting particular images of ourselves. Phonologists should, then, be able to do as speakers do, in identifying and classifying accents, but with a more technical rather than emotional classification of the differences and similarities between them. An accent, in phonological terms, is an idealised system which speakers of that variety share. Although slight differences in its use may be apparent, both across and within individuals, its speakers will still share more in common with one another, and with that idealised accent system, than with speakers of any other idealised accent system. Standard accents should also be described in just the same way as non-standard ones, as they provide just the same sort of social and geographical information about their users: that is, although it is quite common for speakers of a standard accent, such as SSBE in the south of England, to claim that they have no accent, other speakers (and phonologists) know different.

A more detailed appreciation of the cues speakers attend to in different accents, and the social judgements they make on that basis, is a matter for sociolinguistics and dialectology rather than phonology. The main contribution a phonologist can make is to produce a classification of types of differences between accents, which can then be used in distinguishing any set of systems; and that is the goal of this chapter. In the next three sections, then, we shall introduce a three-way classification of accent differences, and illustrate these using examples involving both consonants and vowels. First, the systems of two accents may contain different numbers of phonemes, so different phonemic oppositions can be established for them: these are systemic differences. Second, the same phonemes may have different allophones: these are realisational differences. Finally, there are distributional differences, whereby the same lexical item may have different phonemes in two different varieties; or alternatively, the same phoneme may have a phonological restriction on its distribution in one variety but not another.

8.2 Systemic differences

The first and most obvious difference between accents is the systemic type, where a phoneme opposition is present in one variety, but absent in another. Consonantal examples in English are relatively rare. As we have already seen, some varieties of English, notably SSE, Scots and NZE, have a contrast between /w/ and /ʍ/, as evidenced by minimal pairs like *Wales* and *whales*, or *witch* and *which*. Similarly, SSE and Scots have the voiceless velar fricative /x/, which contrasts with /k/ for instance in *loch* versus *lock*, but which is absent from other accents. NZE speakers will therefore tend to have one more phoneme, and Scots and SSE speakers two more, than the norm for accents of English.

Conversely, some accents have fewer consonant phonemes than most accents of English. For instance, in Cockney and various other inner-city English accents, [h]-dropping is so common, and so unrestricted in terms of formality of speech, that we might regard /h/ as having disappeared from the system altogether. This is also true for some varieties of Jamaican English. In many parts of the West Indies, notably the Bahamas and Bermuda, there is no contrast between /v/ and /w/, with either [w] or a voiced bilabial fricative [β] being used for both, meaning that /v/ is absent from the phonemic and phonetic systems. The same contrast is typically missing in Indian English, but the opposition is resolved in a rather different direction, with the labio-dental approximant [ʋ] very frequently being used for the initial sound of *wine* and *vine*, or *west* and *vest*. Again, there is only a single phoneme in this case in Indian English.

The number of accent differences involving vowels, and the extent of variation in that domain, is very significantly greater than in the case of consonants for systemic, realisational and distributional differences. This probably reflects the fact that the vowel systems of all English varieties are relatively large, so that a considerable number of vowels occupy a rather restricted articulatory and perceptual space; in consequence, whenever and wherever one vowel changes, it is highly likely to start to encroach on the territory of some adjacent vowel. It follows that a development beginning as a fairly minor change in the pronunciation of a single vowel will readily have a knock-on effect on other vowels in the system, so that accent differences in this area rapidly snow-ball. In addition, as we saw in earlier chapters, the phonetics of vowels is a very fluid area, with each dimension of vowel classification forming a continuum, so that small shifts in pronunciation are extremely common, and variation between accents, especially when speakers of those accents are not in day-to-day communication with each other, develops easily.

Systemic differences in the case of vowel phonemes can be read easily from lists of Standard Lexical Sets and the systems plotted from these on vowel quadrilaterals. If for the moment we stick to the four reference accents introduced in the last chapter, namely SSBE, GA, SSE and NZE, we can see that SSBE has the largest number of oppositions, with the others each lacking a certain number of these.

Comparing GA to SSBE, we find that GA lacks /ɒ/, so that LOT words are produced with /ɑː/, as are PALM words, while CLOTH has the /ɔː/ of THOUGHT. In this respect, SSBE is 'old-fashioned': it maintains the ancestral state shared by the two accents. However, in GA realis-ations of the earlier /ɒ/ have changed their quality and merged, or become identical with the realisations of either /ɑː/ or /ɔː/. GA also lacks the centring diphthongs of SSBE, so that NEAR, SQUARE, CURE share the vowels of FLEECE, FACE, GOOSE respectively, but since GA is rhotic, the former lexical sets also have a realisation of /r/, while the latter do not. In this case, however, the historical innovation has been in SSBE. At the time of the initial settlement of British immigrants in North America, most varieties of English were rhotic, as GA still is; but the ancestor of SSBE has subsequently become non-rhotic. The loss of /r/ before a consonant or a pause in SSBE has had various repercussions on the vowel system, most notably the development of the centring diphthongs.

In systemic terms, NZE lacks only one of the oppositions found in SSBE, namely that between /ɪ/ and /ə/; in NZE, both KIT and LETTER words have schwa. There are more differences in symbols between the SSBE and NZE lexical set lists in Chapter 7; but these typically reflect realisational, and sometimes distributional, rather than systemic differ-ences, as we shall see in the next two sections. That is to say, I have chosen to represent the vowel of NZE TRAP as /ɛ/ and DRESS as /e/, FLEECE as /ɪi/ and FACE as /ɛɪ/, to highlight the typical realisational differences between the two accents. However, in phonemic terms, the TRAP and DRESS vowel, and the FLEECE and FACE vowel, still contrast in NZE just as they do in SSBE. That is, the pairs of vowel phonemes in (1) are equivalent: they are symbolised differently because they are very generally pronounced differently (and we could equally well have chosen the same phonemic symbols in each case, to emphasise this parity, at the cost of a slightly more abstract system for NZE; see the discussion in Section 7.2.2 above), but the members of the pairs are doing the same job in the different accents.

(1) SSBE   NZE
     ɛ   e   DRESS
     æ   ɛ   TRAP
     iː   ɪi   FLEECE
     eɪ   ɛɪ   FACE

When we turn to SSE, however, we find a considerably reduced system relative to SSBE. As we might expect, given that SSE is rhotic, it lacks the centring diphthongs, so that NEAR, SQUARE, CURE share the vowels of FLEECE, FACE, GOOSE, though the former will have a final [ɹ] following the vowel. SSE also typically lacks the /ɛː/ vowel of NURSE, with [ʌr] appearing here instead; so the NURSE and STRUT sets share the same vowel. Leaving aside vowels before /r/, however, there are three main oppositions in SSBE which are not part of the SSE system, as shown in (2).

(2) SSBE   SSE
     a   a   TRAP
     ɑː   a   PALM
     ɒ   ɒ   LOT
     ɔː   ɒ   THOUGHT
     ʊ   u   FOOT
     uː   u   GOOSE

Each of these three contrasting pairs of vowel phonemes in SSBE corresponds to a single phoneme in SSE. While *Sam – psalm, cot – caught,* and *pull – pool* are minimal pairs in SSBE, establishing the oppositions between /a/ and /ɑː/, /ɒ/ and /ɔː/, and /ʊ/ and /uː/ respectively, for SSE speakers the members of each pair will be homophonous. There is no vowel quality difference; and the Scottish Vowel Length Rule, which makes vowel length predictable for SSE and Scots, means there is no contrastive vowel quantity either. There is some variation in SSE in this respect: speakers who have more contact with SSBE, or who identify in some way with English English, may have some or all of these oppositions in their speech. If an SSE speaker has only one of these contrasts, it is highly likely to be /a/ – /ɑ/; if /ʊ/ and /u/ are contrasted, we can predict that the /ɒ/ – /ɔ/ and /a/ – /ɑ/ pairs also form part of the system.

Of course, such systemic differences are not restricted to the reference accents surveyed above and in Chapter 7. For instance, within British English, many accents of the north of England and north

Midlands fail to contrast /ʊ/ and /ʌ/, so that *put* and *putt*, or *book* and *buck* all have /ʊ/. In some parts of the western United States, speakers typically lack the /ɑː/ – /ɔː/ opposition found in GA, and will therefore have /ɑː/ in both *cot* and *caught*. Other varieties of English have an even more extreme reduction of the vowel system relative to SSBE. These are typically accents which began life as second language varieties of English: that is, they were at least initially learned by native speakers of languages other than English, although they may subsequently have become official language varieties in particular territories, and be spoken natively by more recent generations. Inevitably, these varieties have been influenced by the native languages of their speakers, showing that language contact can also be a powerful motivating force in accent variation.

One case involves Singapore English. Singapore became a British colony in 1819, and English was introduced to a population of native speakers of Chinese, Malay, Tamil and a number of other languages. Increasingly today, children attend English-medium schools, and use English at home, so that Singapore English is becoming established as a native variety. Its structure, however, shows significant influence from other languages, notably Malay and Hokkien, the Chinese 'dialect' with the largest number of speakers in Singapore. As with many accents, there is a continuum of variation in Singapore English, so that non-native speakers are likely to have pronunciations more distant from, say, SSBE: thus, while a native Singapore English speaker will say [maɪl] 'mile', a second-language speaker who is much more influenced by his native language may say [mʌʊ]. Increasingly, younger speakers of Singapore English are also looking to American rather than British English as a reference variety, so that further change in the system is likely. The system presented as Singapore English (SgE) in (3) is characteristic of native or near-native speakers. Note that SgE has no contrastive differences of vowel length, and that /ɯ/ is the IPA symbol for a high back unrounded vowel.

(3)

SSBE	SgE	Set number	Keyword
ɪ	i	1	KIT
ɛ	ɛ	2	DRESS
a	ɛ	3	TRAP
ɑ	ɔ	4	LOT
ʌ	ʌ	5	STRUT
ʊ	u	6	FOOT
ɑː	ɛ	7	BATH
ɒ	ɔ	8	CLOTH

ɜː	ɯ	9	NURSE
iː	i	10	FLEECE
eɪ	e	11	FACE
ɑː	ʌ	12	PALM
ɔː	ɔ	13	THOUGHT
oʊ	o	14	GOAT
uː	u	15	GOOSE
aɪ	ai	16	PRICE
ɔɪ	ɔi	17	CHOICE
aʊ	au	18	MOUTH
ɪə	iə	19	NEAR
ɛə	ɛ	20	SQUARE
ɑː	ʌ	21	START
ɔː	ɔ	22	NORTH
ɔː	o	23	FORCE
ʊə	uə	24	CURE
ɪ	i	25	HAPPY
ə	ə	26	LETTER
ə	ə	27	COMMA

As (3) shows, many of the vowel oppositions found in SSBE are absent from SgE; and in the great majority of cases, the main reason for the changes in SgE is the structure of other languages spoken in Singapore. (The same contact influences account for realisational differences between SgE and other Englishes, which we consider in the next section.) Looking at the various phoneme mergers in SgE in more detail, we find the patterns in (4).

(4) *Lexical sets*

	Merged SgE vowel	*Malay*	*Hokkien*
DRESS, TRAP, BATH	ɛ	e	e
KIT, FLEECE	i	i	i
LOT, THOUGHT	ɔ		ɔ
FOOT, GOOSE	u	ʊ, u	u
STRUT, PALM, START	ʌ	no low back vowels	

In all these cases, lexical sets which have distinct vowels in SSBE (and often in other accents too) share a single vowel in SgE; and furthermore, this vowel tends to correspond to the vowel found in either Hokkien, or Malay, or both. Thus, instead of /ɛ/ versus /a/, SgE has only /ɛ/; both Hokkien and Malay have only a higher vowel in this area, namely /e/ (and realisationally, SgE /ɛ/ raises to [e] before plosives and affricates, as in *head*, *neck*, neutralising the opposition between /e/, the monoph-thong found in FACE words, and /ɛ/ in TRAP, DRESS in this context, so that *bread – braid, red – raid, bed – bade* are homophones). The merger of the KIT, FLEECE sets follows the pattern for Malay and Hokkien, and the same is true of STRUT/PALM/START; neither Malay nor Hokkien has any low back vowels, and the SgE vowel for all these sets is higher and more central; in SgE this merger means that *cart* and *cut*, or *charm* and *chum*, are homophonous. In the cases of LOT/THOUGHT, and FOOT/GOOSE, SgE follows the Hokkien pattern; Malay has neither /ɒ/ nor /ɔ/, but both /ʊ/ and /u/. Whichever local language has exerted most influence in any particular instance, it is clear that native language systems have acted as a filter or template for non-native learners of Singapore English, creating the vowel system found today.

8.3 Realisational differences

In the second type of accent difference, part of the system of phonemes may be the same for two or more accents, but the realisations of that phoneme or set of phonemes will vary. For instance, in SSBE, SSE and GA, /l/ has two main allophones, being clear, or alveolar [l] before a stressed vowel, as in *light, clear*, but dark, velarised [ɫ] after a stressed vowel, as in *dull, hill*. This distribution of allophones is not the only possibility in English, however. In some accents, /l/ is always realised as clear; this is true, for instance, of Tyneside English (or 'Geordie'), Welsh English, and some South African varieties. On the other hand, in Australia and New Zealand, /l/ is consistently pronounced dark; and indeed, realisations may be pharyngeal rather than velar, or in other words, pronounced with a restriction even further back in the vocal tract. In London English, there is a further allophone of /l/, namely a vocalised (or vowel-like) realisation finally or before a consonant: in *sell, tall, people, help*, /l/ is typically realised as a high or high mid back vowel like [ʊ] or [o]. For younger speakers, vocalisation is also taking hold in medial position, in words like *million*; and the process is also spreading beyond London, as part of the shift towards so-called 'Estuary English', a mixture of SSBE and London English which is arguably becoming a new standard for young people, especially in urban centres in the south of England.

The other English liquid consonant, /r/, also provides plenty of scope for realisational differences. /r/ is typically an alveolar or slightly retro-flex approximant for SSBE and GA, but at least in medial position, is frequently realised as an alveolar tap in SSE (the tap is also a common realisation in South African English). In some parts of the north of England, notably in Northumberland and County Durham, a voiced uvular fricative [ʁ] is quite commonly found, although this may be receding gradually.

In other areas of northern England, this time notably Yorkshire, Tyneside and Liverpool, [ɹ] appears as an allophone of /t/, typically between vowels and across a word-boundary, as in *not on* [nɒɹɒn], *lot of laughs* [lɒɹə …], *get a job* [gɛɹə …]. In Merseyside, voiceless stops are very generally realised as fricatives or affricates in word-final position, so that *cake*, *luck*, *bike* will be [keɪx], [lʊx], [baɪx]: whereas in Scots and SSE the appearance of [x] in *loch* constitutes a systemic difference, as there are minimal pairs establishing an opposition of /x/ and /k/, in Liverpool the velar fricative is clearly an allophone of /k/, so that the accent difference between, say, SSBE and Merseyside English in this respect is realisational, but not systemic.

Turning to vowels, one particularly salient example involves the FACE and GOAT vowels, which in SSBE, NZE and Australian English are pronounced consistently as diphthongs. In GA, the FACE vowel is diphthongal, while the GOAT vowel may be a monophthong; and in SSE and SgE, both are monophthongal, with the predominant allophones being high-mid [e] and [o] in both accents. The NURSE vowel in SSBE is mid central [ɜː]; the same phoneme in NZE is very generally rounded, while in SgE it is typically raised to high-mid back unrounded [ɤ], or high back unrounded [ɯ] (as we might expect, Hokkien has [ɤ], Malay has both [ɤ] and [ɯ], but both lack [ɜ]).

Sometimes, although these realisational differences have no direct impact on the phoneme system, they do lead to neutralisations of otherwise consistent contrasts. For instance, we saw in the last section that SgE speakers raise /ɛ/ to [e] before plosives and affricates; the monophthongal pronunciation of /e/ as [e] in FACE words, and the lack of any systematic vowel-length distinction in SgE means that the contrast of /ɛ/ and /e/ is suspended in this context, leading to identical pronunciations of *bread* and *braid*, or *wreck* and *rake*. It is also possible for realisational differences in vowels to lead to allophonic differences in consonants. For instance, right at the beginning of this book, we identified an allophonic difference between velar [k] and palatal [c], with the latter appearing adjacent to a front vowel. In SSBE, SSE and GA, this will mean that velar realisations will be produced in *cupboard* and *car*, palatals in *kitchen* and *keys*. However, the distribution differs in other varieties of English, depending on their typical realisations of the FLEECE and KIT vowels. In NZE, FLEECE has a high front diphthong, so that *keys* will still have [c]; but no fronting will take place in *kitchen*, since the KIT set in NZE has central [ə]. On the other hand, in Australian English, KIT has a rather high, front [i] vowel so that *kitchen* will certainly attract a palatal [c]; but in some varieties at least, the diphthong in *keys* is central [əɪ], which will therefore favour a velar allophone of /k/.

8.4 Distributional differences

Distributional differences fall into two subclasses. First, there are differences in lexical incidence: certain individual lexical items will simply have one vowel phoneme in some accents, and another in others. For example, British English speakers are quick to comment on American English /aʊ/ in *route*, or /ɛ/ in *lever*; Americans find British English /ruːt/ and /liːvə(ɹ)/ equally odd. Some Northern English English speakers have /uː/ rather than /ʊ/ in *look* and other <oo> words; and it is fairly well-known in Britain that words containing /ɑː/ vary in English English, with *grass, dance, bath*, for instance, having /a/ for many northern speakers, but /ɑː/ in the south, though both varieties have /ɑː/ in *palm*. Similarly, in SSE, *weasel* has /w/, and *whelk* /ʍ/; but in Borders Scots, where these phonemes also contrast, and where indeed most of the same minimal pairs (like *Wales* and *whales*, *witch* and *which*) work equally well, the lexical distribution in these two words is reversed, with /ʍ/ in *weasel* and /w/ in *whelk*.

On the other hand, a difference in the distribution of two phonemes may depend on the phonological context rather than having to be learned as an idiosyncracy of individual lexical items. For instance, in GA there is a very productive restriction on the consonant /j/ when it occurs before /uː/. Whereas in most British English [j] surfaces in *muse, use, fuse, view, duke, tube, new, assume*, in GA it appears only in the first four examples, and not in the cases where the /uː/ vowel is preceded by an alveolar consonant. There is also, as we have seen, a very clear division between rhotic accents of English, where /r/ can occur in all possible positions in the word (so [ɹ], or the appropriate realisation for the accent in question, will surface in *red, bread, very, beer, beard, beer is*), and non-rhotic ones, where /r/ is permissible only between vowels (and will be pronounced in *red, bread, very, beer is*, but not the other cases).

Again, vowels follow the same patterns. For instance, in many varieties of English, schwa is only available in unstressed positions, in *about, father, letter*; in NZE, however, its range is wider, since it appears also in stressed syllables, in the KIT lexical set. Similarly, in some varieties words like *happy* have a tense /i/ vowel in the second, unstressed syllable; this is true for Tyneside English, SSE, GA and NZE. In SSBE, however, only lax vowels are permitted in unstressed syllables, so that /ɪ/ appears in *happy* instead. Not all these distributional restrictions have to do with stress; some are the result of other developments in the consonant or vowel systems. For instance, the presence of the centring diphthongs before historical /r/ in SSBE (and other non-rhotic accents) means that non-low monophthongs cannot appear in this context. On the other hand, in rhotic accents like SSE and GA, there are no centring diphthongs, and the non-low monophthongs consequently have a broader range, with the same vowel appearing in FLEECE and NEAR, FACE and SQUARE, GOOSE and CURE.

In defining how accents differ, then, we must consider all three types of variation: systemic, realisational, and distributional. Although some of these (notably the systemic type) may seem more important to a phonologist, since they involve differences in the phoneme system, we must remember that one of the phonologist's tasks is to determine what speakers of a language know, and how their knowledge is structured. It follows that we must be able to deal with the lower-level realisational and distributional differences too, since these are often precisely the points native speakers notice in assessing differences between their own accent and another variety of English. In any case, all of these types of variation will work together in distinguishing the phonological systems of different accents, and as we have seen, variation at one level very frequently has further implications for other areas of the phonology.

Exercises

1. Plot your vowel system on a vowel quadrilateral. (You may wish to use one diagram for monophthongs, and one for diphthongs; or even more than one for diphthongs if you have a system with a large number of these.)

2. What is your phonemic consonant system? Provide minimal pairs to establish the contrasts involved. Pay particular attention to whether your accent is rhotic or non-rhotic, and whether your system includes /ʍ/ and /x/ or not. Do any of the consonant phonemes of SSBE fail to contrast in your accent? Why might this be?

3. Set out the differences between your variety, for both vowel and consonant systems, and (a) SSBE, (b) GA, (c) SSE, (d) NZE, (e) SgE. In each case, classify the discrepancies as systemic, realisational, or distributional. If you are a non-native speaker of English, or bilingual in English and another language, can you identify aspects of your native language(s) which might be responsible for some of the differences you have identified?

Recommendations for reading

Giegerich (1992) provides phonological analyses of some of the varieties discussed here; characteristics of an overlapping set of accents are also discussed in Carr (1999). Much of the data discussed here comes from Wells (1982), which covers a fairly complete range of varieties of English, although the Singapore English material is mainly from Tan (1998). Trudgill (2000) provides more detail on the dialects of England in particular, and Wolfram and Schilling-Estes (1996) on American English. More theoretical discussion of dialectology and sociolinguistics respectively can be found in Chambers and Trudgill (1980) and Hudson (1995). If you are interested in the history of English, a good introductory survey is Graddol, Leith and Swann (1996).

9 Syllables

9.1 Phonology above the segment

At the end of the last chapter, we returned to the central issue, and the central task for phonologists, of assessing what speakers know about the structure of their language. In this book so far, we have concentrated on this knowledge, and the speech production that reflects it, at the level of the segment and below. That is, we have discussed vowels and consonants, the features of which they are composed and the judgements speakers make about them. However, as we shall see in this chapter and the next, speakers' behaviour and intuitions also indicate the presence of phonological organisation at a series of higher levels, above the single segment. Vowels and consonants are not just strung together haphazardly into long, unstructured strands: instead, they form a series of larger units with their own internal structure and distribution, governed by their own rules.

The first and smallest of these superordinate units, the syllable, will be the main focus of this chapter. Recognising and understanding syllables helps us state some phonological processes (for example involving English /l/ and the aspiration of voiceless plosives) more accurately and succinctly. As we shall see in Chapter 10, the syllable and the next unit, the foot, are also crucial in analysing and determining the position of stress within each word. Finally, in whole utterances consisting of a sentence or more, phonological processes may apply between words, and rhythm and intonation produce the overall melody of longer stretches of speech.

9.2 The syllable

Speakers certainly have an intuitive notion of how many syllables each word contains: for instance, speakers of English would generally agree that *meadow*, *dangerous* and *antidisestablishmentarianism* (allegedly the longest word in the language) have two, three and twelve syllables respectively. It is less easy for speakers to reflect consciously on the internal structure of syllables, or to decide where one stops and the next starts; but a wide variety of cross-linguistic studies have helped phonologists construct a universal template for the syllable, within which particular languages select certain options. The internal structure of the syllable, and evidence for its subparts from a range of English phonological processes, will be the topic of this chapter.

9.3 Constituents of the syllable

The universal syllable template accepted by most phonologists is given in (1). Note that small sigma (σ) is shorthand for 'syllable'; capital sigma (Σ), as we shall see later, is used to symbolise the foot.

(1)

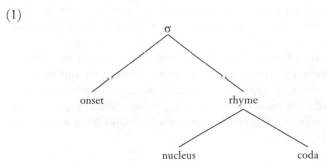

The only compulsory part of the syllable, and hence its head, or most important, defining unit, is the nucleus. This will generally contain a vowel (and recall that vowels are [+syllabic]): indeed, the syllable *I*, or the first syllable of *about*, consist only of a nucleus. If no vowel is available, certain consonants can become nuclear, and play the part of a vowel. In English, this is true of /l/, /m/, /n/, and /r/ in rhotic accents: that is, the sonorant consonants, in natural class terms. Each of the words *bottle, bottom, button, butter* has two syllables, and in each case, the second syllable consists only of nuclear, or syllabic [l̩], [m̩], [n̩] and [ɹ̩].

Both the onset and the coda are optional constituents, and each, if filled, will contain one or more consonants. In English, *be* has an onset but no coda; *eat* has a coda but no onset; and *beat* has both. Recognising the difference between the nucleus, which is primarily the domain of vowels, and the onset and coda, where we find consonants, also casts some light on the relationship between the high vowels /i u/ and the glides /j w/. Phonetically, it is very hard to detect any systematic difference between [i] and [j], or [u] and [w] respectively; however, we can now say that [i] and [u] are [+syllabic], while the glides are [−syllabic], so that in *ye*, [j] is in the onset and [iː] in the nucleus, and similarly in *woo*, [w] is an onset consonant and [uː] a nuclear vowel. Clearly, [j] and [iː] are extremely similar phonetically; furthermore, since distinguishing syllable peaks, or nuclei, from margins allows us to predict where each will occur, they are in complementary distribution (and the same is true of [w] and [uː]). This makes [j] and [iː], and [w] and [uː], allophones of a single phoneme, with their distribution determined by position in the syllable.

9.4 The grammar of syllables: patterns of acceptability

Patterns of permissibility vary in terms of filling these constituents of the syllable. In some languages, like Arabic, every syllable must have an onset; if a word without an onset in one syllable is borrowed from another language, for instance, a glottal stop [ʔ] will be inserted to meet that requirement. Conversely, in Hawaiian, no codas are allowed, so that coda consonants in loanwords will be deleted, or have an extra, following vowel introduced, so the consonant becomes an onset and therefore legal. However, there do not seem to be any languages which either insist on codas, or rule out onsets. The universal, basic syllable type is therefore CV: all known languages allow this, whether they have other, more complex syllable types in addition, or not.

9.4.1 Phonotactic constraints

Even languages like English, which allow both onsets and codas, have restrictions on the permissible contents of those slots: these restrictions are known as phonotactic constraints. In particular, English allows clusters of two or three consonants in both onsets and codas; some languages have more complex cluster types, others only CC, and perhaps in the onset only. Some restrictions on the composition of clusters reflect structural idiosyncrasies of English; these include the examples in (2).

(2) In a CCC onset, C_1 must be /s/.
    /ŋ/ does not appear in onsets.
    /v ð z ʒ/ do not form part of onset clusters.
    /t d θ/ plus /l/ do not form permissible onset clusters.
    /h/ does not appear in codas.
    Coda clusters of nasal plus oral stop are only acceptable if the two stops share the same place of articulation.
    /lg/ is not a permissible coda cluster.

9.4.2 The Sonority Sequencing Generalisation

However, some other restrictions on possible clusters are not specific to English, but rather reflect universal prohibitions or requirements. The most notable phonological principle which comes into play here is known as the Sonority Sequencing Generalisation, and governs the shape of both onsets and codas. Sonority is related to the difference between sonorants (sounds which are typically voiced, like approximants, nasal stops and vowels) and obstruents (oral stops and fricatives, which may be either voiced or voiceless). Sonorants are more sonorous; that is, their acoustic properties give them greater carrying power. If you stood at the front of a large room and said one sound as clearly as you could, a listener at the back would be much more likely to be able to identify a highly sonorous sound like [ɑ] than a sound at the other end of the sonority range, such as [t].

Our knowledge of acoustic phonetics and other aspects of sound behaviour can be combined to produce a sonority scale like the one given in (3). Here, the most sonorous sounds appear at the top, and the least sonorous at the bottom. Some English examples are given for each category.

(3) Low vowels   [ɑ æ] ...
    High vowels   [i u] ...
    Glides   [j w]
    Liquids   [l ɹ]
    Nasals   [m n ŋ]
    Voiced fricatives   [v z] ...
    Voiceless fricatives [f s] ...
    Voiced plosives   [b d g]
    Voiceless plosives [p t k]

Natural classes of sounds which function together in phonological processes are often composed of single or adjacent levels on the sonority hierarchy. For instance, English liquids and nasals can be syllabic, and these are the closest consonants to the vowel series (with the exception of the glides; and as we have seen already, we might say that [j w] do have syllabic counterparts, namely the high vowels).

The general rule expressed by the Sonority Sequencing Generalisation is that syllables should show the sonority curve in (4).

(4)

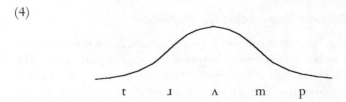

t   ɹ   ʌ   m   p

The nucleus constitutes the sonority peak of the syllable, with sonority decreasing gradually towards the margins. In syllables like *trump, prance, plant,* the outermost consonants, at the beginning of the onset and the end of the coda, are at the bottom end of the sonority scale, while less marginal consonants, adjacent to the vowel, are also closer to the vowel in their sonority value. Lack of adherence to the Sonority Sequencing Generalisation therefore rules out onsets like *[lp], *[jm], *[ɹg], although onsets with the same segments in the opposite order are found in *play, muse, grey.* Similarly, universal sonority restrictions mean English lacks *[pm], *[kl], *[mr] codas, although again clusters with the opposite order, which do show descending sonority, are attested in *lamp, silk, harm* (the last in rhotic accents only).

Like many rules, the Sonority Sequencing Generalisation has an exception, and this involves the behaviour of /s/. The onset clusters in *spray, skew* have the sonority profile in (5).

(5)

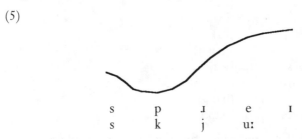

s   p   ɹ   e   ɪ
s   k   j   uː

That is, the marginal consonant [s] has a higher sonority value than the adjacent voiceless plosive: yet there is no question of drawing a syllable boundary here and recognising two syllables within the same word, as [s] is not one of the English consonants which can become nuclear, or syllabic. The same problem arises in codas. We would normally use a sonority pattern like the one in (6a) to tell us that a syllable division should be made, giving two syllables in *little,* but one in *lilt.* However, codas with both orders of clusters involving [s] are possible, as in *apse* and *asp,* or *axe* and *ask;* and the same sonority pattern in (6b) must be analysed, contrary to the Sonority Sequencing Generalisation, as corresponding to a single syllable.

(6)

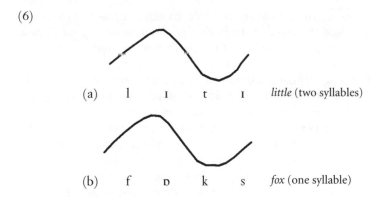

(a)   l   ɪ   t   ɪ   *little* (two syllables)

(b)   f   ɒ   k   s   *fox* (one syllable)

These exceptions are at least not random: cross-linguistically, violations of the Sonority Sequencing Generalisation always seem to involve coronal consonants (those produced using the tongue tip or blade, and typically alveolars), and especially /s/. Such consonants seem to behave exceptionally in a number of ways, and have to be excluded from various phonological generalisations, though it is not yet quite clear why.

9.5 Justifying the constituents

9.5.1 Syllable-based processes

Recognising the syllable as a phonological unit, and moreover a unit with the internal structure hypothesised in (1), allows us to write improved versions of some phonological rules introduced in previous chapters. Sometimes, what determines or conditions a phonological process or change is simply the nature of an adjacent segment: for example, we have seen that the nasal of the prefix *in-* assimilates to a following consonant, and that sounds frequently become voiced between other voiced segments. However, in other cases it is the position of a sound within the syllable that dictates its phonetic shape. In turn, improvements in our statement of phonological rules may help justify or validate the constituents we have proposed for the syllable.

First, the notion of the syllable in general, and the onset constituent in particular, helps us to state the environment for aspiration of voiceless stops more accurately. Our current, rather informal version predicts aspiration in absolute word-initial position; as we already know, /p t k/ surface as aspirated in *pill*, *till*, *kill*, but not when preceded by /s/ in *spill*, *still*, *skill*. However, this is not the whole story, since we can also observe aspiration in *repair*, *return*, *record*, though not in *respond*, *disturb*, *discard*. In these examples, the voiceless stops are medial, not initial in the word: but in *repair, return, record*, they are the sole constituents of the onset for syllable two, and therefore initial in that syllable. As for *respond, disturb, discard*, here also /p t k/ are part of the onset, but this time preceded by /s/; and since a preceding /s/ inhibits aspiration in onsets word-initially, we should not be surprised that the same pattern is found in onsets word-medially. In short, aspiration of voiceless stops takes place, not at the beginning of the word, but at the beginning of the onset.

Similar support can be found for the second major constituent of the syllable, namely the rhyme. As we have seen already, many varieties of English have two main allophones of /l/, clear or alveolar [l] and dark, velarised [ɫ], in complementary distribution. However, stating the nature of this complementarity is not entirely straightforward. In earlier chapters, the rule for velarisation of /l/ was informally stated as taking place after the vowel in a word, giving the correct results for *clear* versus *hill*, for instance. This works well enough when we are only dealing with word-initial versus word-final clusters, but it leaves a grey area in word-medial position, where we find dark [ɫ] in *falter, hilltop*, but clear [l] in *holy, hilly*. Again, this is resolvable if we state the rule in terms of the syllable: clear [l] appears in onset position, and dark [ɫ] in the coda. In fact, this process does not only provide evidence for the contrast between onset and coda position, but for the superordinate rhyme constituent, which consists of the nucleus plus the optional coda. In cases of consonant syllabification, where /l/ (or another sonorant consonant) comes to play the role of a vowel and therefore occupies the nuclear position, as in *bottle, little*, we find the dark allophone. /l/-velarisation, then, takes place in syllable rhymes, as shown in (7).

(7)

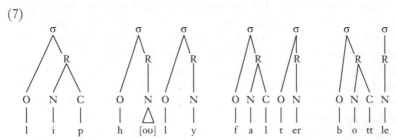

9.5.2 Onset Maximalism

Of course, this rule (and similarly the earlier reformulation of aspiration in syllable terms) will only work appropriately if we are drawing the boundaries between syllables, and therefore determining what consonants are in the coda of an earlier syllable, and which in the onset of a later one, in the right way. We have already noted that the Sonority

Sequencing Generalisation provides one guide to drawing syllable boundaries; leaving aside the exceptional case of /s/ in clusters, we find that legal syllables exhibit a sonority profile which ascends from the left-hand margin of the onset, up to a sonority peak in the nucleus, and subsequently descends to the right-hand margin of the coda, as shown in (4) above. However, there is another, equally important principle governing syllable division, namely Onset Maximalism (also known as Initial Maximalism), which is set out in (8).

(8) *Onset Maximalism*
   Where there is a choice, always assign as many consonants as poss-ible to the onset, and as few as possible to the coda. However, remember that every word must also consist of a sequence of well-formed syllables.

Onset Maximalism tells us that, in a word like *leader*, the medial /d/ must belong to the second syllable, where it can be located in the onset, rather than the first, where it would have to be assigned to the less favoured coda. This is a permissible analysis, because both [liː] and [də(ɹ)] are well-formed syllables of English: think of *lea*, or *Lee*, and the first syllable of *dirty*, or *Derwent*. The same goes for a word like *oyster*, where both parts of the medial /st/ cluster belong to the onset of the second syllable, while the initial diphthong forms a syllable on its own. There are many monosyllabic words with initial /st/, like *stop, start, stitch, stoop*, and if /st/ make a well-formed onset word-initially, then they can combine to make a well-formed onset word-medially, too.

We can use the same sort of argument to account for the alternation between dark [ɫ] in *hill*, but clear [l] in *hilly*. Since *hill* has only a single syllable, and moreover has a vowel occupying the nuclear slot, the /l/ must necessarily be in the coda, and is therefore dark. However, in *hilly*, there are two syllables, and Onset Maximalism means /l/ must be in the onset of the second, where it automatically surfaces as clear. This kind of alternation, where the form that surfaces depends on its position in the syllable, is quite common in English and other languages. For instance, in non-rhotic accents of English, /r/ has two realisations, namely [ɹ] in onsets, and zero in codas: it surfaces in *red, bread, very*, but not in *car, park*. Again, as with the alternation between clear and dark variants of /l/, we find that the addition of suffixes can change the situation: so for instance, *star* has no final consonant for non-rhotic speakers, but there is a medial [ɹ] in *starry*, where the /r/ constitutes the onset of the second syllable. It also follows that syllable boundaries will not always coincide with morpheme boundaries, or boundaries between meaningful units: in *starry*, the two morphemes are *star*, the stem, and -*y*, the suffix, but the syllables are divided as *sta.rry* (note that a dot signals a syllable boundary). As we shall see in more detail in the next chapter, similar alternations arise across word boundaries in connected speech: thus, although *car* has no final [ɹ], and the same is true of *car keys*, where the second word begins with a consonant, in *car engine* the second word begins with a vowel, and the /r/ can be allocated to the onset of that syllable, where it duly surfaces as [ɹ]. As far as native speakers' knowledge goes, there are two ways of analysing this. We could assume that speakers store *car* mentally as /kɑr/, and delete the /r/ before a consonant or pause. Alternatively, the entry in the mental lexicon or dictionary might be /kɑ/, with [ɹ] being inserted before vowels. Choices of this kind, and their implications, are vitally important for phonologists; but pursuing the issue here is beyond the scope of this book.

However, in a word like *falter*, we cannot straightforwardly assign the medial /lt/ to the second syllable. The Sonority Sequencing Generalisation would allow the syllable boundary to follow /lt/ (compare *fault*, a well-formed monosyllabic word), but Onset Maximalism forces the /t/ at least into the onset of the next syllable. The syllable boundary cannot, however, precede the /l/ because /lt/ is not a possible word-initial cluster in English, and it consequently cannot be a word-internal, syllable-initial cluster either. On the other hand, in *bottle* our immediate reaction might be to proposed *bo.ttle*, which fits both the Sonority Sequencing Generalisation and Onset Maximalism. However, we then face a problem with the first syllable, which would on this analysis consist only of /bɒ/; and, as we shall see in Chapter 10, a single short vowel cannot make up the rhyme of a stressed syllable. The first syllable clearly needs a coda; but *bott.le* is not quite right either, since native speakers, asked to check syllable boundaries by saying each syllable in the word twice, typically say *bot-bot-tle-tle*. The same is true of other words with the same problematic structure, like *syllable* in fact, which comes out as *syl-syl-la-la-ble-ble*; it may not be coincidental that these are written with double medial consonants. The usual solution here is to analyse the /t/ of *bottle* as ambisyllabic: that is, as belonging simultaneously in both the coda of the first syllable, and the onset of the second. This does not conflict with either the Sonority Sequencing Generalisation or Onset Maximalism, but also accords with native speakers' intuitions and the stress patterns of English.

9.5.3 *Literary applications of syllable constituents*

Recognising the onset and rhyme does not only allow us to write more accurate versions of our phonological rules, and to understand alternations between sounds which arise when we add an affix or combine words into longer strings, thus creating different syllabifications. These two constituents are also integral parts of two rather different literary traditions. In alliterative poetry, the important constituent is the onset, which must be identical in several words in a single line (and often, the more the better). An example from the Scots poetic tradition appears in (9); this is a short excerpt from the late fifteenth or early sixteenth century 'Flyting of Dunbar and Kennedie'. A flyting is essentially a long string of insults, here hurled by each of the poets named in the title at the other, in turn. The use of alliteration, which is clear even from the two lines given, extends throughout the fairly lengthy poem.

(9) Conspiratour, cursit cocatrice, hell caa   (caa = crow)
     Turk, trumpour, traitour, tyran intemperate ...

It is clear that almost all of the words in the first line begin with <c> /k/, and those in the second with <t> /t/; and in some cases, here *cocatrice, intemperate*, the alliterating sound may appear in word-internal onset positions too. More obviously, or at least more familiarly, the rhyme of the syllable determines poetic rhyme: for a perfect rhyme, the nucleus and coda (if any) must be exactly the same, though whether there is an onset or not, or what it is, does not matter. That is, *meet* rhymes with *eat*, and with *beat*, and with *sweet*; but it does not rhyme with *might* or *mate*, where the nucleus is different; or with *bee*, where there is no coda; or with *leek* or *beast*, where there is a coda, but not one consisting of the single consonant /t/.

9.5.4 Syllable weight

There is one further aspect of syllable structure which provides evidence for the syllable-internal structure set out above. Here again, as in the case of poetic rhyme, the nucleus and coda seem to work together, but the onset does not contribute at all.

In fact, there are two further subdivisions of syllable type, and both depend on the structure of the rhyme. First, syllables may be closed or open: a closed syllable has a coda, while in an open syllable, the rhyme consists of a nucleus alone, as shown in (10). It does not matter, for these calculations, whether the nucleus and coda are simple, containing a single element, or branching, containing more than one: a branching nucleus would have a long vowel or diphthong, while a branching coda would contain a consonant cluster.

(10)

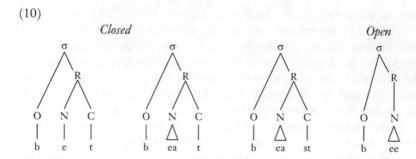

There is a second, related distinction between light and heavy syllables. A light syllable contains only a short vowel in the rhyme, with no coda, as in the first syllable of *potato, report, about*. Although the first two cases have onsets, and the third does not, all these initial syllables are still light, because onsets are entirely irrelevant to the calculation of syllable weight. If a syllable has a complex rhyme, then it is heavy; and complexity can be achieved in two different ways. First, a heavy syllable may have a short vowel, but one or more coda consonants, as in *bet, best*. Second, it may have a branching nucleus, consisting of a long vowel or diphthong; such a syllable will be heavy whether it also has a filled coda, as in *beast, bite*, or not, as in *bee, by*.

As we shall see in detail in the next chapter, syllable weight is a major factor in determining the position of stress in a word: essentially, no stressed syllable in English may be light. This means that no lexical word, or full word of English can consist only of a short vowel alone, with or without an onset, since such words, including nouns, verbs and adjectives, must be able to bear stress: thus, we have *be, say, loss*, but not *[bɪ], *[sɛ], *[lɒ]. On the other hand, function words like the indefinite article *a*, or the pronunciation [tə] for the preposition *to*, which are part of the grammatical structure of sentences and are characteristically unstressed, can be light. In cases where these do attract stress, they have special pronunciations [eɪ] and [tuː], where the vowel is long, the nucleus branches, and the syllable is therefore heavy.

There is one set of cases where a conflict arises between syllable weight on the one hand, and the guidelines for the placement of syllable boundaries on the other: we have already encountered this in the discussion of *bottle* above. In most cases, these two aspects of syllable structure work together. For instance, *potato, report, about* each have a consonant which could form either the coda of the first syllable, or the onset of the second. Onset Maximalism would force the second analysis, placing the first [t] of *potato*, the [p] of *report*, and the [b] of *about* in onset position; this is supported by the evidence of aspiration in the first two cases. The first syllable of each word is therefore light; and since all three syllables are unstressed, this is unproblematic. Similarly, in words like *penny, follow, camera, apple*, Onset Maximalism would argue for the syllabifications *pe.nny, fo.llow, ca.me.ra*, and *a.pple*. However, in these cases the initial syllable is stressed, in direct contradiction of the pervasive English rule which states that no stressed syllable may be light. In these cases, rather than overruling Onset Maximalism completely, we can regard the problematic medial consonant as ambisyllabic, or belonging simultaneously in the coda of the first syllable and the onset of the second. It therefore contributes to the weight of the initial, stressed syllable; but its phonetic realisation will typically reflect the fact that it is also in the onset of the second syllable. Consequently, as we saw earlier, the /l/ in *hilly, follow* appears as clear, as befits an onset consonant, while /r/ in *carry* is realised as [ɹ], its usual value in onset position, rather than being unpronounced, its usual fate in codas.

Exercises

1. Mark the syllable boundaries in the following words. In each case, what led to your decision in placing the boundary there? You should consider the contribution of the Sonority Sequencing Generalisation, Onset Maximalism, and syllable weight.

    danger, unstable, anxious, discipline, narrow, beyond, bottle, bottling

2. Draw syllable trees for each of the words from Exercise 1. In each case, and for each syllable, mark the Onset, Rhyme, Nucleus and Coda; indicate whether any of these constituents branch; and note any cases of ambisyllabicity.

3. Make a list of all the two consonant clusters which are ruled out by the Sonority Sequencing Generalisation in (a) onset and (b) coda position. For each one, try to think of an apparent exception in word-medial position, where in fact the first consonant of the apparent 'cluster' belongs in the coda of syllable one, and the second in the onset of syllable two. For example, sonority rules out final [kn]; an apparent (but not real) exception would be *acknowledge*.

4. Make a list of at least five consonant clusters which are ruled out either by the Sonority Sequencing Generalisation, or by the phonotactic rules of English, but for which you can find actual exceptions which do contain these clusters. These may be recent loan words or foreign names. For example, English does not generally allow /ʃ/ in onset clusters, but

a number of borrowings from Yiddish, like /ʃtʊm/, /ʃtɪk/, do have these clusters.

Recommendations for reading

Carr (1999), Giegerich (1992), Hogg and McCully (1987) and Spencer (1996) all discuss the phonology of the syllable in much more detail than is possible in this chapter. Information on the syllable from a phonetic point of view can be found in Catford (1988), Ladefoged (1993) and Couper-Kuhlen (1986).

10 The word and above

10.1 Phonological units above the syllable

Native speakers who are not linguists may be slightly surprised by the discovery, discussed in the last chapter, that they can count syllables and determine the boundaries between them. However, they will typically be much more consciously aware of the word as a linguistic unit, probably because words are meaningful units; moreover, in a highly literate society, we are familiar with orthographic words, which conveniently appear with white space on each side. Individual spoken or written words can also appear in isolation: three of the four conversational turns in (1) consist, entirely appropriately and comprehensibly, of single words.

(1) A: Did you find a babysitter?
  B: Yes.
  A: Who?
  B: Denise.

However, words, like other linguistic units, are not entirely straightforward and trouble-free for native speakers or for linguists. In particular, there are cases where it is difficult to determine how many words we are dealing with. For example, is *washing-machine* one word or two? Is it easier or more difficult to decide if we write it as *washing machine*, without the hyphen? And if we conclude that this is two words, then where does that leave *teapot*, where two acceptable independent words seem to make up one larger one? It seems that compounds like this take some time to become accepted in the speech community as single words: for a while, they appear as two written words, though signalling one distinct concept semantically (thus, a *washing-machine* washes clothes, not dishes, for which we have *dishwashers*, or cars, which go through a *carwash*). As they are encountered more commonly, they begin to be written with a hyphen, which ultimately drops to leave a single orthographic word – although speakers may think of a compound as a single word before this stage is reached. Conversely, although *didn't, can't* or *it's* appear as single written words, speakers will tend to regard these as sequences of two words, contracted by the deletion of a vowel, as signalled by the apostrophe. So, *it's* (in *It's Saturday*) is a short form of *it is*, and therefore in a sense two words, as distinct from *its* (in *The cat ate its dinner*), which is a single word however you look at it.

For phonological purposes, we can simply note these tricky exceptional cases, and accept that native speakers typically have a good intuitive idea of what a word is (although this is an issue of considerable interest to morphologists). What we are interested in are the phonological properties of words; and the most important of these, in English at least, is stress. As we shall see, although each word has its own characteristic stress pattern when uttered in isolation, words are generally produced in strings, combining into phrases and whole sentences; and phonological processes also operate at these higher levels. First, the position of stress on the isolated word may change when that word forms part of a larger unit; and secondly, some segmental processes, affecting vowels or consonants, may also apply between words.

10.2 Stress

10.2.1 The phonetic characteristics of stress

Native speakers of English are intuitively aware that certain syllables in each word, and one syllable in particular, will be more phonetically prominent than others. In *father*, the first syllable seems stronger than the second; in *about*, it is the other way around; and in *syllable*, the first syllable stands out from the rest. These more prominent syllables are stressed; and stress is a culminative property, signalled by a number of subsidiary phonetic factors, which work together to pick out a stressed syllable from the unstressed ones which surround it. There are three important factors which combine to signal stress. First, the vowels of stressed syllables are produced with higher fundamental frequency; that is, the vocal folds vibrate more quickly, and this is heard as higher pitch. Secondly, the duration of stressed syllables is greater, and they are perceived as longer. Thirdly, stressed syllables are produced with greater intensity, and are thus heard as louder than adjacent unstressed syllables. In addition, stress has effects on vowel quality, in that vowels often reduce to schwa under low stress. To take our earlier examples of *father*, *about*, and *syllable*, the stressed syllables have the full vowels [ɑː], [aʊ] and [ɪ] respectively, but the unstressed ones typically have schwa; we do not say [sɪlæbɛl], for instance, but [sɪləbəl] (or [sɪləbl̩]).

The interaction of these phonetic factors produces an effect which is clearly audible, but crucially relative: that is, we cannot distinguish a stressed from an unstressed syllable if each is spoken in isolation, but only by comparing the syllables of a word, or a longer string, to see which are picked out as more prominent. Indeed, within the word, there can be more than one level of stress. Some words have only stressed versus unstressed syllables, as in *father*, *about* and *syllable*. However, in *entertainment*, the first and the third syllables bear some degree of stress. Both have full vowels [ε] and [eɪ], as opposed to the unstressed second and fourth syllables with schwa; but the third syllable is more stressed than the first. Phonologists distinguish primary stress (the main stress in the word, on the third syllable of *entertainment*) from secondary stress (a lesser degree of stress elsewhere, here initially). Special IPA diacritic marks are placed at the beginning of the relevant syllable to show primary and secondary stress, as in *entertainment* [ˌɛntə'teɪnmənt], *about* [ə'baʊt], and *father* ['fɑːðə]. The difference between secondary stress and no stress is clear in a pair like *raider* ['ɹeɪdə(ɹ)], where the second syllable is unstressed and has schwa, versus *radar* ['ɹeɪˌdɑ(ɹ)], where both syllables have full vowels and some degree of stress, although in both words the first syllable is more stressed than the second.

10.2.2 Predicting stress placement

The languages of the world fall into two broad classes in terms of stress position. In fixed-stress languages, primary stress always (or virtually always) falls on one particular syllable; thus, in Scots Gaelic, main stress is consistently initial, except in some English loanwords, such as *buntata* 'potato', where stress stays on the syllable it occupies in the source language (here, the second). Similarly, stress in Swahili consistently falls on the penultimate syllable of the word. On the other hand, languages may have free stress, like Russian; here, words which differ semantically may be identical in terms of phonological segments, and differ only in the position of stress, as in Russian *'muka* 'torment' versus *mu'ka* 'flour'.

This division into fixed and free-stress languages is relevant to phonologists because it has a bearing on how children learning the language, and adults using it, are hypothesised to deal with stress. In a fixed-stress language, we can assume that children will learn relatively quickly and easily that stress placement is predictable, and will formulate a rule to that effect; if they encounter exceptions to the rule, they may overgeneralise the regular pattern, and have to unlearn it in just those cases, so that a child acquiring Scots Gaelic may well produce *'buntata* temporarily for English-influenced *bun'tata*. This is precisely like the situation with other regular linguistic processes, like the regular morphological plural rule adding -*s* to nouns, which children typically overgeneralise to give *oxes, mouses, tooths* at an early stage, before learning the appropriate form of these irregular nouns individually. In free-stress languages, on the other hand, part of language acquisition involves learning that the position of stress is not predictable, but instead has to be memorised as part of the configuration of each individual word, along with the particular combination of vowels and consonants that make it up. There are no stress rules: instead, speakers are assumed to have a mental representation of each word with stress marked on it.

English does not fall fully within either class: it is neither a wholly fixed-stress, nor a wholly free-stress language. This is in large part a result of its peculiar history. English inherited from Germanic a system with fixed stress falling on the first syllable of the stem; but it has subsequently been strongly influenced by Latin, French and other Romance languages, because of the sheer number of words it has borrowed. It has therefore ended up with a mixture of the Germanic and Romance stress systems. On the one hand, there are pairs of words which contrast only by virtue of the position of stress, such as *con'vert, pro'duce* (verb) vs. *'convert, 'produce* (noun). This initially makes English look like a free stress language, like Russian, but turns out to reflect the fact that such stress rules as English has vary depending on the lexical class of the word they are applying to. On the other hand, there are some general rules, as in (2), which do allow stress placement to be predicted in many English words.

(2) a. Noun rule: stress the penultimate syllable if heavy. If the penultimate syllable is light, stress the antepenult.
a.'ro.ma   a.'gen.da   'di.sci.pline

b. Verb rule: stress the final syllable if heavy. If the final syllable is light, stress the penultimate syllable.
o.'bey   u.'surp   a.'tone   'ta.lly   'hu.rry

These stress rules depend crucially on the weight of the syllable: recall from the last chapter that a syllable will be heavy if it has a branching rhyme, composed of either a long vowel or diphthong, with or without a coda, or a short vowel with a coda. A syllable with a short vowel and no coda will be light. As (2a) shows, English nouns typically have stress on the penultimate syllable, so long as that syllable is heavy, which it is in *aroma* (with a long [oː] vowel or a diphthong [oʊ] depending on your accent), and in *agenda*, where the relevant vowel is short [ɛ], but followed by a consonant, [n]; this must be in the coda of syllable two rather than the onset of syllable three, since there are no *[nd] initial clusters in English. However, in *discipline* the penultimate syllable is light [sɪ]; the following [pl] consonants can both be in the onset of the third syllable, since there are initial clusters of this type in *play, plant, plastic* and so on. Since [sɪ] has only a short vowel and no coda consonants, it fails to attract stress by the Noun Rule, and the stress instead falls on the previous, initial syllable.

A similar pattern can be found for verbs, but with stress falling consistently one syllable further to the right. That is, the Verb Rule preferentially stresses final syllables, so long as these are heavy. So, *obey* (with a final long vowel or diphthong), has final stress, as do *usurp* (having a final syllable [ɜːp] for SSBE, with a long vowel and a coda consonant, and [ʌɹp] for SSE, for instance, with a short vowel and two coda consonants), and *atone* (with a long vowel or diphthong plus a consonant in the coda). However, both *tally* and *hurry* have final light syllables, in each case consisting only of a short vowel in the rhyme. It follows that these cannot attract stress, which again falls in these cases one syllable further left.

These stress rules are effective in accounting for stress placement in many English nouns and verbs, and for native speakers' actions in determining stress placement on borrowed words, which are very frequently altered to conform to the English patterns. However, there are still many exceptions. A noun like *spaghetti*, for instance, ought by the Noun Rule to have antepenultimate stress, giving ˈ*spaghetti*, since the penultimate syllable [gɛ] is light; but in fact stress falls on the penultimate syllable, following the original, Italian pattern – in English, the <tt> is of course pronounced as a single [t], not as two [t]s or a long [t]. Although the Noun Rule stresses penultimate or antepenultimate syllables, nouns like *machine, police, report, balloon* in fact have final stress. There are also cases where the stress could, in principle, appear anywhere: in *catamaran*, for instance, the stress pattern is actually ˈcatamaˌran, with primary stress on the first syllable and secondary stress on the final one, again in contradiction of the Noun Rule, which would predict caˈtamaran (as in Deˈcameron), with antepenultimate stress as the penult is light. There is equally no good reason why we should not find ˌcataˈmaran (as in ˌAldeˈbaran); while another logical possibility, ˌcatamaˈran, has a pattern more commonly found in phrases, such as ˌflash in the ˈpan, or ˌDesperate ˈDan. It seems that the Noun Rule and Verb Rule are misnomers; these are not really rules, though they do identify discernible tendencies.

Leaving aside the question of predictability, we can certainly describe the position of stress on particular words accurately and clearly using tree diagrams. In these diagrams, which form part of a theory called Metrical Phonology, each syllable is labelled either S or W: and because stress, as we saw above, is not an absolute but a relative property of syllables, these labels do not mean 'Strong' and 'Weak', but 'Stronger than an adjacent W' and 'Weaker than an adjacent S', respectively. Some illustrative trees are shown in (3).

(3)

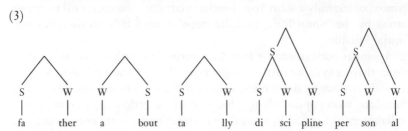

Trees of this sort allow us to compare different words at a glance and tell whether their prominence patterns, and thus the position of stress, are the same or not; from (3), we can see that *father* and *tally* share the same stress pattern, though *about* has the relative prominence of its two syllables reversed. This is particularly important for longer words with more syllables, where prominence patterns are naturally more complex; so, (3) also shows that *discipline* and *personal* have the same stress patterns. Note that, even in longer words, metrical trees can only branch in a binary way: that is, each higher S or W node can only branch into two lower-level constituents, never more. This is straightforward enough for disyllabic words like *father*, *about* and *tally*; but in *discipline*, *personal*, tree construction involves two steps. Initially, the first two nodes are put together; then the higher-level S node these form is in turn combined with the leftover W syllable, to form another binary unit. This kind of pattern can be repeated in even longer words.

In cases involving both primary and secondary stresses, these trees are particularly helpful: (4) clearly shows the different patterns for *entertainment* and *catamaran*. In particular, the trees allow us easily to identify the main stress of each word, which will always be on the syllable dominated by nodes marked S all the way up the tree.

(4)

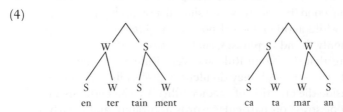

Finally, metrical trees are useful in displaying the stress patterns of related words. In English, as in many other languages, stress interacts with the morphology, so that the addition of particular suffixes causes stress to shift. Most suffixes are stress-neutral, and do not affect stress placement at all: for instance, if we add -*ise* to '*atom*, the result is '*atomise*; similarly, adding -*ly* to '*happy* or '*grumpy* produces '*happily*, '*grumpily*, with stress remaining on the first syllable. However, there are two other classes of suffixes which do influence stress placement. The first are stress-attracting suffixes, which themselves take the main stress in a morphologically complex word: for example, adding -*ette* to '*kitchen*, or -*ese* to '*mother*, produces ₍*kitchen'ette*, ₍*mother'ese*. Other suffixes, notably -*ic*, -*ity* and adjective-forming -*al*, do not become stressed themselves, but cause the stress on the stem to which they attach to retract one syllable to the right, so that '*atom*, e'*lectric* and '*parent* become a'*tomic*, *elec'tricity* and *pa'rental*. The varying stress patterns of related words like *parent* and *parental* can very straightforwardly be compared using tree diagrams, as in (5).

(5)

 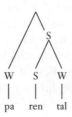

S	W
pa	rent

W	S	W
pa	ren	tal

There is one final category of word with its own characteristic stress pattern. In English compounds, which are composed morphologically of two independent words but signal a single concept, stress is characteristically on the first element, distinguishing the compounds '*greenhouse* and '*blackbird* from the phrases *a* ₍*green* '*house*, *a* ₍*black* '*bird*. Semantically too, the difference is obvious: there can be brown blackbirds (female blackbirds are brown), or blue greenhouses, but *The* ₍*green* '*house is blue* is semantically ill-formed. In phrases, the adjectives *black* and *green* are directly descriptive of the noun, and have to be interpreted that way; on the other hand, the meaning of compounds are not determined compositionally, by simply adding together the meanings of the component parts, so that *greenhouse* signals a particular concept, with no particular specification of colour. Stress is clearly crucial in marking this difference between compounds and phrases; in noting it, however, we are already moving beyond the word, and into the domain of even larger phonological units.

10.3 The foot

So far we have been assuming that syllables group into words, with some words being composed of only a single syllable. Strictly, however, the word is not a phonological unit, but a morphological and syntactic one; and as we shall see in the next section, phonological processes are no great respecters of word boundaries, operating between words just as well as within them. The next biggest *phonological* unit above the syllable is the foot.

The normally accepted definition is that each phonological foot starts with a stressed syllable (though we shall encounter an apparent exception below), and continues up to, but not including, the next stressed syllable. This means that *cat in a hat* consists of two feet, the first containing *cat in a*, and the second, *hat*. Although *cat flap* consists of only two words (or indeed one, if we agree this is a compound), as opposed to four in *cat in a hat*, it also consists of two feet, this time one for each syllable, since both *cat* and *flap* bear some degree of stress. Indeed, because English is a stress-timed language, allowing approximately the same amount of time to produce each foot (as opposed to syllable-timed languages, like French, which devote about the same amount of time to each syllable regardless of stress), *cat in a hat* and *cat flap* will have much the same phonetic duration. The same goes for *the cat sat on the mat*, with rather few unstressed syllables between the stressed ones, and as *snug as a bug in a rug*, with a regular pattern of two unstressed syllables to each stress. This isochrony of feet, whereby feet last for much the same time regardless of the number of syllables in them, is responsible for the characteristic rhythm of English.

Like syllables, feet can also be contrasted as stronger and weaker. Sometimes, there will be more than one foot to the word; for instance, as we saw earlier, a word like '*raider*, with primary stress on the first syllable and no stress on the second, can be opposed to '*ra͵dar*, with primary versus secondary stress. It is not possible to capture this distinction using only syllable-based trees, since both *raider* and *radar* have a stronger first syllable and a weaker second syllable. However, these two W nodes are to be interpreted in two different ways, namely as indicating no stress in *raider*, but secondary stress in *radar*. To clarify the difference, we must recognise the foot. *Raider* then has a single foot, while *radar* has two, the first S and the second W. Recall that small sigma (σ) indicates a syllable, and capital sigma (Σ), a foot.

(6)

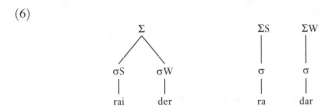

In other cases, the same number of feet may be spread over more than one word, so that *'cat flap* has two feet, related as S versus W, while *,cat in a 'hat* also has two feet, although here the first foot is larger, including *in a* as well as *cat*, and the prominence relationship of W S reflects the fact that *cat flap* is a compound bearing initial primary stress, while *cat in a hat* is a phrase, with main stress towards the end.

Feet can also be classified into types, three of which are shown in (7). The iambic type, structured W S, contradicts the claim above that all feet begin with a stressed syllable; but in fact, at the connected speech level, the first, unstressed syllable in such cases will typically become realigned, attaching to the preceding foot. So, in *cup of tea*, the weak syllable *of* will be more closely associated with the preceding stronger syllable, with which it then forms a trochaic foot, than with the following one, as evidenced by the common contraction *cuppa* for *cup of*.

(7) *Trochee (trochaic foot)*

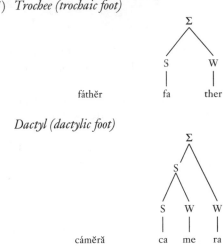

Iamb (iambic foot)

These foot types are important in scansion, or analysing verse. For example, the blank verse of Shakespeare's plays involves iambic pentameters: each line has five iambic feet, as shown in the metre of two lines from *The Merchant of Venice* (8).

(8) Thĕ quálítỹ ŏf mércỹ ís nŏt stráined
     Ĭt dróppĕth ás thĕ géntlĕ ráin frŏm héaven

To take a less exalted example, (9) shows two lines with rather different metrical structure. The first consists of two dactyls and a final 'degenerate' foot composed of a single stressed syllable. Note that a foot of this kind, like *dock* here, or any monosyllabic word like *bit, cat* in normal conversation, cannot really be labelled as S or W: since stress is relational, it requires comparison with surrounding feet. The second line is again made up of iambic feet.

(9) Híckŏrỹ díckŏrỹ dóck
     Thĕ móuse răn úp thĕ clóck.

Finally (taking another nursery rhyme, since these often have particularly clear and simple metre), a line like *Márỹ, Márỹ quíte cŏntrárỹ* is composed of four trochaic feet.

Poetry also provides an excellent illustration of the English preference for alternating stress. It does not especially matter whether we have sequences of SWSWSWSW, or SWWSWWSWWSWW; but what does matter is avoiding either lapses, where too many unstressed syllables intervene between stresses, or clashes, where stresses are adjacent, with no unstressed syllables in between at all. The English process of Iambic Reversal seems designed precisely to avoid stress clashes of this kind. It affects combinations of words which would, in isolation, have final stress on the first word, and initial stress on the second. For instance, (10) shows that the citation forms (that is, the formal speech pronunciation of a word alone, rather than in a phrase) of *thirteen* and *champagne* have final stress.

(10) A: How many people turned up?
      B: ˌThirˈteen.

A: What are you drinking?
B: Cham'pagne.

However, when final stressed words like *thirteen* and *champagne* form phrases with initial-stressed ones like *players* or *cocktails*, the stress on the first word in each phrase moves to the left, so that in *'thir,teen 'players* and *'cham,pagne 'cocktails*, both words have initial stress. This is clearly related to the preference of English speakers for eurhythmic alternation of stronger and weaker syllables, as illustrated in (11).

(11)

W S	S W		S W	S W
thirteen	players	→	thirteen	players

W S	S W		S W	S W
champagne	cocktails	→	champagne	cocktails

If these words retained their normal stress pattern once embedded in the phrases, we would find clashing sequences of WSSW, as shown on the left of (11), in violation of eurhythmy; consequently, the prominence pattern of the first word is reversed, changing from an iamb to a trochee – hence the name Iambic Reversal. The result is a sequence of two trochaic feet, giving SWSW and ideal stress alternation.

It is also possible, however, for the normal stress patterns of words to be disrupted and rearranged in an altogether less regular and predictable way, reflecting the fact that stress is not only a phonological feature, but can also be used by speakers to emphasise a particular word or syllable. If one speaker mishears or fails to hear another, an answer may involve stressing both syllables in a word, in violation of eurhythmy: so, the question *What did you say?* may quite appropriate elicit the response *'thir'teen*. Similarly, although phrases typically have final stress, a speaker emphasising the first word may well produce the pattern *a 'cat in a 'hat*, rather than *a ,cat in a 'hat*. This is partly what makes the study of intonation, the prominence patterns of whole utterances, so complicated. It is true that there is a typical 'tune' associated with each utterance type in English: for instance, questions typically have raised pitch towards the end of the sentence, while statements have a pitch shift downwards instead. However, the stress patterns of particular words (which may themselves be altered for emphasis) interact with these overall tunes in a highly complex and fluid way.

Furthermore, speakers can use stress and intonation to signal their attitude to what they are saying; so that although *No* spoken with slightly dropping pitch signals neutral agreement, it may also be produced with rising pitch to signal surprise, or indeed with rising, falling, and rising intonation, to show that the speaker is unsure or doubtful. In addition, intonation is just as subject to change over time, and under sociolinguistic pressures, as any other area of phonology. To take one case in point, there is currently a growing trend for younger women in the south-east of England in particular to extend to statements the high rising tune characteristic of questions, so that *She's going out* and *She's going out?* will have the same characteristic intonation pattern for these speakers. Whatever the source of this innovation (with the influence of Australian television soaps like *Neighbours* being a favourite popular candidate), it shows that intonation is not static, and that there is no single, necessary connection between particular patterns and particular utterance types. These complexities, combined with the fact that the analysis of intonation has its own (highly complex and often variable) technical terms and conventions, mean that it cannot be pursued further here.

10.4 Segmental phonology of the phrase and word

10.4.1 Phrase-level processes

Although the main focus of this chapter has inevitably been on stress and prominence, this is not the only phonological characteristic of the word and phrase levels: segments may also be affected by those adjacent to them. The bulk of these segmental phonological processes are characteristic of fast and casual speech, and are often referred to as connected speech processes (CSPs for short). These generally involve either assimilations (whereby two adjacent sounds become more similar in quality, as the articulations used to produce them become more similar), or reductions; both these process types are natural consequences of talking more quickly and perhaps less carefully. Most CSPs are also optional, and will tend to be suspended or at least occur less frequently in more formal situations and in slower speech. To take just two examples, when two adjacent words have final and initial stops, these typically come to share the same place of articulation, so that *sit close* will tend to have medial [kk], and *odd message* [bm]. Function words like *he, than, you, my* also frequently reduce to [ɪ], [ðən] (or even [ən]), [jə], [mə]: all these component processes, notably loss of consonants (in *he, than*), shortening of vowels (in *he* again), and reduction of vowels to schwa (in *than, you, my*) as a result of loss of stress, are segmental weakenings.

Speaking quickly and informally will also tend to cut the duration of unstressed vowels in full lexical words like nouns, verbs and adjectives, with a concomitant effect on their quality. In words like *deduce, profound, connect*, the first syllable in careful speech may contain a full vowel, [i], [aʊ] or [ɒ] respectively; but in faster speech and more relaxed circumstances, these are highly likely to be reduced to schwa. Work by Fry in 1947 reported that nearly 11 per cent of vowel phonemes in English consisted of /ə/, with its nearest rival, at 8 per cent, being /ɪ/, the other vowel frequently found in unstressed syllables. To put this in perspective, all other vowels in the survey fell below 3 per cent. This indicates clearly how common unstressed syllables were in 1947; and they are not likely to have reduced in frequency since. In some cases, however, vowels do not only reduce in fast speech: they are deleted. A word like *connect*, in connected speech, could be pronounced either as [kənɛkt] or [knɛkt]; and in cases like this one, and *potato* [pteɪtoʊ], the result actually violates the phonotactics of English, since *[kn] and *[pt] are not permissible clusters.

Such processes do not always affect vowels, however: sometimes both vowels and consonants are elided in fast speech, so that whole syllables may vanish when we compare the citation forms of words like *February*, *veterinary* with their fast speech equivalents, [fɛbɹi], [vɛʔnɹi]. Note also [ʔ] for /t/ in the second example; reduction of a stop to a glottal stop, or indeed to a fricative, is another example of lenition or weakening. Moreover, phonological reductions and assimilations across word boundaries typically affect consonants rather than vowels. For example, at the phrase level, word-final /s/ followed by word-initial /j/ often combine to produce [ʃ], so that *race you* is often [ɹeɪʃə], not the citation form [ɹeɪs ju]. In this case, a very similar process also takes place word-internally, resulting in medial [ʃ] in *racial*; but again typically, these word-internal cases are not so clearly optional, and [ɹeɪsjəl] would tend to be seen as old-fashioned or an example of a speaker trying too hard to speak 'correctly'. Another very common process applying between words is [ɹ]-intrusion in non-rhotic accents of English, where [ɹ] appears between [ɑ], [ɔ], or [ə] and another following vowel, although there is no <r> in the spelling and no etymological /r/ in the word concerned. For instance, the name of a tennis tournament, the *Stella Artois event*, will typically in casual speech be pronounced as [ðəstɛləɹɑtwɑɹəvɛnt], with intrusive [ɹ] after both cases of <a>; and similarly, we find well-known examples like *the idea is* [ðiaɪdiəɹɪz] and *law and order* [lɔɹənɔdə]. Again, this process also takes place within words, as in *sheep baa*[ɹ]*ing*, *draw*[ɹ]*ing*, *magenta*[ɹ]*ish*. This might, on the face of it, seem a rather unusual fast speech process, since it involves the addition of a segment; but producing two vowels side-by-side appears to be rather difficult for speakers, and an intrusive consonant may allow more fluid and less hesitant speech. Many of these processes therefore have a similar rationale, in making life easier for speakers, and allowing speech tempo to be kept consistently fast.

10.4.2 Word-internal morphophonological processes

However, there is another class of segmental phonological processes. In contrast to the connected-speech processes discussed above, these do not apply across word boundaries, but are rather confined within words, where they tend to take place in response to the addition of a particular suffix – generally those suffixes identified as causing stress retraction in 10.2.2. Forms with these suffixes are also prone to odd and irregular segmental processes. For instance, when the suffix -*ity* is added to *electric*, the final [k] of *electric* becomes [s] in *electricity*. The same suffix may also alter the stem vowel: when -*ity* is added to *divine, sane, serene*, the long stressed vowels of the stems are shortened in *divinity, sanity, serenity*. These changes are also unlike CSPs in that it is often hard to see why they take place where they do: while a fast speech reduction or assimilation is generally a response to speed of speech, and involves ease of articulation pressures, the word-internal type typically creates an alternation between two independent phonemes, not directly motivated by the phonological context (as in the /k/ and /s/ of *electric* – *electricity*). Even where there does seem to be a reduction, as in the shortening of the stressed vowel in *divine* to *divinity* on the addition of the -*ity* suffix, it is not obvious why this particular suffix should have this effect; and it cannot be ascribed to speed of speech, since these morphophonological processes are obligatory, regardless of speed of speech or sociolinguistic factors: hence, the citation forms of *electricity, divinity* will also show these changes.

Although the affixes which provoke these segmental changes generally also influence the position of stress, this is not always the case. For instance, adding the past tense marker -*t* or -*d* to irregular verbs like *keep* – *kept, sleep* – *slept, leap* – *leapt* has no effect on stress, but does seem to cause a categorical shortening of the stem vowel. One of the most important jobs for phonologists, bearing in mind the focus discussed throughout this book on what speakers know about their language, and what they must be assumed to do in order to learn, produce and understand it, is to work out where to draw the line between productive processes which speakers apply regularly and which they will generalise to new forms in the language, and fossilised processes which might have started out as regular phonetic developments, perhaps CSPs, in the history of the language, but which are now simply associated with individual words or small groups of words. That is, perfectly natural phonetic processes may in time become less transparent, and less regular. In the case of *keep* – *kept*, or *divine* – *divinity*, we must ask ourselves whether the processes of vowel shortening, which perhaps were regular and phonetically motivated centuries ago, are still part of native speakers' active knowledge of English, and still involve those speakers in actual processes of adding suffixes and shortening vowels; or whether children must learn that words like *keep* and *divine* have related, but different forms which are stored separately and produced on appropriate syntactic occasions. Since phonology, like all other areas of language, is consistently undergoing change and development, with new processes constantly arising and different accents diverging, our only definite conclusion can be that today's connected-speech processes will present tomorrow's phonologists with exactly the same problem.

Exercises

1. Look back at the English stress rules presented in (2). Consider the adjectives *lovely, beautiful, surreal, high-pitched, scarlet, noisy, sensible.* On the basis of these forms, do you think adjectives typically follow the Noun Rule or the Verb Rule? Is there a single, general pattern for adjectives at all?

2. Draw metrical S W trees for the following words:

person, personal, personality, elephant, peninsula, disentanglement

In each case, make sure that the syllable which carries main stress is dominated by S all the way up the tree.

3. Find examples of English words which consist of the following foot structures:

one iamb	one trochee
one dactyl	one iamb followed by one trochee
one dactyl followed by one trochee	

4. Find some examples of poems which contain mainly iambic, trochaic and dactylic feet. Make a metrical analysis of several lines from each, using diacritics like *cát* over a stressed syllable, and *ŏf* over an unstressed one, to show what the foot structure is.

5. Transcribe the following utterances in citation form and as appropriate for faster, more casual speech. In each case, say what connected speech processes you might expect to find in the second rendition:

I expect he has gone to meet her
Helen had a banana and a bread cake

Recommendations for reading

Carr (1999), Giegerich (1992), Roach (2001) and Spencer (1996) all provide further information on the complexities of English stress, while Couper-Kuhlen (1986), Cruttenden (1986) and Roach (2001) give detailed descriptions of English intonation and its analysis. A more theoretical approach to intonation is reported in Ladd (1996). The difference between phonological processes which interact with the morphology and those which are closer to the phonetics forms the basis of Lexical Phonology; Kaisse and Shaw (1995) provide a helpful outline of this model.

Discussion of the exercises

Chapter 2

1. Explaining these pronunciations involves two steps: first, figure out what the relevant environments are; and second, try to work out why the learner is producing these pronunciations in those environments. In terms of environments, [d] appears word-initially and word-finally, and [ð] medially, between vowels; [ʃ] appears before or after an [ɪ] vowel, and [s] next to other vowels. Since we know the speaker in this case is a learner of English, our first attempt at explanation might involve the patterns of her native language: we can hypothesise that in that language, [d] and [ð] are allophones of a single phoneme, and likewise [ʃ] and [s] are allophones of a single phoneme, with a distribution like the one our learner imposes on English.

Predicted pronunciations would be: *Daddy* [dæði]; *either* [ð]; *loathe* [d]; *ship* [ʃ]; *pass* [s]; *dish* [ʃ]; *usher* [s].

2. One list of minimal pairs for initial position would be *my* – *nigh* – *pie* – *buy* – *tie* – *die* – *guy* – *lie* – *rye*. You can add *me* – *key* in a slightly different context. You should be able to produce similar lists medially and finally; what you won't find are cases of initial [ŋ], final [h], or for some speakers at least, final [r].

3. The main point here is that some pairs of sounds are in complementary distribution in this language: notably, voiced and voiceless pairs of sounds ([g] – [k], [b] – [p], [z] – [s]) do not contrast, since the voiced one appears initially and medially, and the voiceless one finally. Linguist A has noticed this, and uses a single symbol for each pair; Linguist B uses different graphs. Linguist A also uses a single symbol for [ŋ], which is a single consonant in this language, and represents [h] with <h> each time it is pronounced. Linguist B uses <ng> for [ŋ], making it look like two consonants, and has no symbol for [h] word-finally. In short, A is using a system designed for this particular language; B is following English patterns, and is probably a native speaker of English.

Chapter 3

1. (a) hang, ship, foot, sit
   (b) nap, jug, knock, lot, jump
   (c) nap, hang, jug, bet, lamb
   (d) pot, sad, boss, size, hen, call
   (e) wash, hall, red, yellow

2. (a) They are all approximant consonants
   (b) They are all voiceless
   (c) They are all fricatives.

3. (a) A: nasal, and voiced   B: oral, and voiceless
   (b) A: fricatives   B: plosives
   (c) A: voiced   B: voiceless

4. Note that ALL these consonants are pulmonic and egressive; and all are central except for [l].

[sɑːm]	voiceless alveolar fricative; voiced bilabial nasal stop
[dʒɛstə]	voiced postalveolar affricate; voiceless alveolar fricative; voiceless alveolar plosive; and for some speakers, a final [r] = voiced alveolar central approximant
[wɪtʃ] or [ʌɪtʃ]	voiced labial-velar approximant, or voiceless labial-velar fricative; voiceless postalveolar affricate
[klaɪm]	voiceless velar plosive; voiced alveolar lateral approximant; voiced bilabial nasal stop
[hɛvɪ]	voiceless glottal fricative; voiced labio-dental fricative
[splɪnt]	voiceless alveolar plosive; voiceless bilabial plosive; voiced alveolar lateral approximant; voiced alveolar nasal stop; voiceless alveolar plosive
[lɒk] or [lɒx]	voiced alveolar lateral approximant; voiceless velar plosive, or voiceless velar fricative
[bɔt]	voiced bilabial plosive; voiceless alveolar plosive
[skwɛltʃ]	voiceless alveolar plosive; voiceless velar plosive; voiced labial-velar approximant; voiced alveolar lateral approximant; voiceless postalveolar affricate.

Chapter 4

1. These rules are written to say that /d/ becomes [ð] between vowels, and /s/ becomes [ʃ] either before or after [ɪ]. You may if you wish also

write a rule to say explicitly where [d] and [s] appear (e.g. [d] occurs word-initially and word-finally).

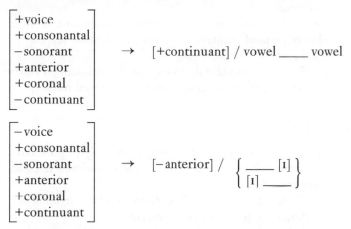

$$
\begin{bmatrix}
+\text{voice} \\
+\text{consonantal} \\
-\text{sonorant} \\
+\text{anterior} \\
+\text{coronal} \\
-\text{continuant}
\end{bmatrix}
\rightarrow \quad [+\text{continuant}] \ / \ \text{vowel} \underline{\quad\quad} \text{vowel}
$$

$$
\begin{bmatrix}
-\text{voice} \\
+\text{consonantal} \\
-\text{sonorant} \\
+\text{anterior} \\
+\text{coronal} \\
+\text{continuant}
\end{bmatrix}
\rightarrow \quad [-\text{anterior}] \ / \ \left\{ \begin{array}{l} \underline{\quad\quad}\ [\text{I}] \\ [\text{I}]\ \underline{\quad\quad} \end{array} \right\}
$$

2. You need a single rule to say that voiced obstruents (you needn't specify the place or whether these are continuants, to cover all the sounds involved) become voiceless at the ends of words.

$$
\begin{bmatrix}
+\text{voice} \\
+\text{consonantal} \\
-\text{sonorant}
\end{bmatrix}
\rightarrow \quad [-\text{voice}] \ / \ \underline{\quad\quad}\#
$$

3. /l/ is   [−syllabic, +consonantal, +sonorant, +continuant, +voice, +lateral, −nasal, +anterior, +coronal, −delayed release, −strident]

   /r/ is   [−syllabic, +consonantal, +sonorant, +continuant, +voice, −lateral, −nasal, +anterior, +coronal, −delayed release, −strident]

   /p/ is   [− syllabic, +consonantal, −sonorant, −continuant, −voice, −lateral, −nasal, +anterior, −coronal, −delayed release, −strident]

   /d/ is   [−syllabic, +consonantal, −sonorant, −continuant, +voice, −lateral, −nasal, +anterior, +coronal, −delayed release, −strident]

   /s/ is   [−syllabic, +consonantal, −sonorant, +continuant, −voice, −lateral, −nasal, +anterior, +coronal, −delayed release, +strident]

   /θ/ is   [−syllabic, +consonantal, −sonorant, +continuant, −voice, −lateral, −nasal, +anterior, +coronal, −delayed release, −strident]

/ŋ/ is   [−syllabic, +consonantal, +sonorant, −continuant, +voice,
         −lateral, +nasal, −anterior, −coronal, −delayed release,
         −strident]

/ʤ/ is   [−syllabic, +consonantal, −sonorant, −continuant, +voice,
         −lateral, −nasal, +anterior, +coronal, +delayed release,
         +strident]

/w/ is   [−syllabic, −consonantal, +sonorant, +continuant, +voice,
         −lateral, −nasal, +anterior, −coronal, −delayed release,
         −strident]

4. Redundant features are:

/l/   everything except [+lateral] −/l/ is the only English lateral
/r/   [−syllabic, +continuant, +voice, −nasal, −delayed release,
       −strident]
/p/   [−syllabic, −lateral, −nasal, −delayed release, −strident]
/d/   [−syllabic, −lateral, −nasal, −strident]
/s/   [−syllabic, −lateral, −nasal, −delayed release]
/θ/   [−syllabic, −lateral, −nasal, −delayed release]
/ŋ/   everything except [+nasal, −anterior, −coronal]
/ʤ/   everything except [+voice, +delayed release]
/w/   [−syllabic, +continuant, +voice, −nasal, −delayed release,
       −strident]

5. (a) the odd one out is [b]; the class is [−syllabic, +sonorant, −nasal]
   (b) the odd one out is [ð]; the class is [−nasal, −continuant]
   (c) the odd one out is [k]; the class is [+anterior, +coronal, −delayed
        release]

6. In two-consonant clusters with [s] as the first consonant, the second
may be a voiceless stop; a liquid; a nasal; a glide. The natural classes
are [−voice, −nasal, −continuant] for the voiceless stops, and [−syllabic,
+sonorant] for the others.

   In three-consonant clusters with [s] as the first consonant, the second
must be a voiceless stop (see above), and the third a liquid or glide
(= [−syllabic, +sonorant, −nasal]).

Chapter 5

1. You should be producing lists like the one in Exercise 2, Chapter 2.
Defective distributions will involve initial [h], final [ŋ], and final [r] if
you are a speaker of a non-rhotic accent.

2. (a) Using only the criteria of predictability of occurrence and invari-

ance of meaning, [ɹ] is in complementary distribution with both [ɹ̥] and [l̩], and [l] with both [ɹ̥] and [l̩].

(b) The usual decision would be to assign [ɹ] and [ɹ̥] to /r/, and [l] and [l̩] to /l/, on the grounds of phonetic similarity.

(c) $\begin{bmatrix} -\text{syllabic} \\ +\text{sonorant} \\ -\text{nasal} \end{bmatrix}$ → [−voice] / [−voice] ____

3. There is no single answer here; it depends on the example you choose. However, there are some analysed models in the chapter.

4. In word-final position, the usual three-way contrast of the voiceless stops is neutralised, and all three are realised by the glottal stop. It would be appropriate to recognise an archiphoneme here; we could use the symbol /P/, /T/ or /K/. Since the three voiceless stop phonemes /p/, /t/ and /k/ are usually distinguished by their place of articulation, the archiphoneme would be specified as [−voice, −nasal, −continuant] (the feature values the voiceless stops share), but would have no value for [anterior] or [coronal].

Chapter 6

1. (a) put, hook, grew, hoe, hold
   (b) see, seat, met, tap, tape
   (c) see, seat, list, through
   (d) about, luck, purse, father (second syllable)
   (e) put, look, food

2. (a) they are all mid vowels
   (b) they are all high front vowels
   (c) they are all diphthongs
   (d) they are all long, high vowels

3. The diagrams here will follow the pattern of (6.15). For /aɪ/, /aʊ/, the arrow will start at low central, and move up to either high front, or high back. For /eɪ/, /oʊ/, the end points are the same, but the start points are high-mid front and high-mid back respectively. Centring diphthongs will all end at schwa.

4. *father*   long low back unrounded; short mid central unrounded
   leaving   long high front unrounded; short high front unrounded
   hear   centring diphthong; first element is short high front unrounded, second is short mid central unrounded. Speakers of rhotic varieties will have a long high front

	unrounded monophthong (plus [r]).
thoroughly	short low-mid central unrounded; short mid central unrounded; short high front unrounded
fast	long low back unrounded; for northern speakers, front rather than back
haste	diphthong, with first element high-mid front unrounded, and second element high front unrounded; or high-mid front unrounded monophthong
lookalike	short high back rounded; short mid central unrounded; diphthong, with first element low central unrounded, and second element high front unrounded
sausage	short low-mid back rounded; short mid central unrounded
ooze	long high back rounded.

Chapter 7

1.

	SSBE	GA	SSE	NZE
water	/wɔːtə/	/wɔːtər/	/wɒtər/	/wɔːtə/
grass	/grɑːs/	/græs/	/gras/	/graːs/
righteousness	/raɪtʃəsnɛs/	/raɪtʃəsnɛs/	/rʌɪtʃəsnɛs/	/raɪtʃəsnɛs/
holiday	/hɒlɪdeɪ/	/hɑːlɪdeɪ/	/hɒlɪde/	/hɒlədeɪ/
pilchard	/pɪltʃəd/	/pɪltʃɜrd/	/pɪltʃʌrd/	/pəltʃəd/
following	/fɒloʊɪŋ/	/fɑloʊɪŋ/	/fɒloɪŋ/	/fɒləuɪŋ/
northeast	/nɔːθiːst/	/nɔrθiːst/	/nɒrθist/	/nɔːθɪist/
spoonful	/spuːnfʊl/	/spuːnfʊl/	/spunful/	/spəunfʊl/

2. (a)
$$\begin{bmatrix} +\text{syllabic} \\ +\text{front} \\ +\text{round} \end{bmatrix} \rightarrow [-\text{round}] \quad / \underline{\quad} \begin{bmatrix} -\text{syllabic} \\ -\text{anterior} \\ -\text{coronal} \end{bmatrix}$$

(b)
$$\begin{bmatrix} +\text{syllabic} \\ -\text{consonant} \\ +\text{sonorant} \end{bmatrix} \rightarrow [-\text{voice}] \quad / \underline{\quad} \begin{bmatrix} -\text{syllabic} \\ -\text{voice} \end{bmatrix}$$

(c)
$$\begin{bmatrix} +\text{syllabic} \\ +\text{high} \\ -\text{mid} \end{bmatrix} \rightarrow [+\text{mid}] \quad / [-\text{syllabic}] \begin{bmatrix} -\text{syllabic} \\ +\text{nasal} \end{bmatrix} \underline{\quad}$$

(d)
$$\begin{bmatrix} +\text{syllabic} \\ -\text{high} \\ -\text{mid} \\ +\text{back} \end{bmatrix} \rightarrow \begin{bmatrix} +\text{high} \\ +\text{round} \end{bmatrix} / \left\{ \begin{array}{l} \#\underline{\quad} \\ \underline{\quad} \begin{bmatrix} -\text{syllabic} \\ -\text{anterior} \\ +\text{coronal} \end{bmatrix} \end{array} \right\}$$

3. No specific answers can be given here, since there is too wide a choice of possible examples. However, consulting the tables (3) and (4) in Chapter 7 should help.

4. Again, this exercise depends on your accent, so no answers can be provided. In deciding which symbols to use, you should again consult tables (3) and (4) in Chapter 7, and may find it helpful to talk through your reasoning with fellow-students who have both similar and different accents.

Chapter 8

All the exercises in this chapter have a wide range of possible answers, depending on your particular accent. The advice for Exercise 4, Chapter 7 above may again be helpful in approaching these tasks. Before you begin, you should be sure you are confident about the differences between systemic, realisational and distributional variation.

Chapter 9

1. *dan.ger*   Onset Maximalism might suggest *da.nger*, but there are no *[ndʒ] initial clusters in English.

   un.sta.ble   [st] is a permissible initial cluster; *[nst] is not, so the syllable division must be between [n] and [s]. However, note that [s] is higher in sonority than [t], so there is a violation of the Sonority Sequencing Generalisation. In the third syllable, [l] is the nucleus (or for speakers who have a schwa vowel in this syllable, the coda).

   an[k.ʃ]*ious*   Final [ŋk] is common in English (*thank, sink* ...), but not initial *[kʃ].

   discipline   On the grounds of Onset Maximalism, the syllabification should be *di.sci.pline*, but then the first two syllables would be light, and the first is stressed. There is likely to be ambisyllabicity between the first and second syllables therefore, giving *dis.sci.pline*.

   nar.row   Another case of ambisyllabicity.

   be.yond   Here, the first syllable is unstressed and can be light; the glide [j] can therefore be in the onset of the second syllable only, prioritising Onset Maximalism.

   bot.tle   Another case of ambisyllabicity. It is true that there are no cases of onset *[tl-] clusters in English; but note that the syllabic [l] here is in the nucleus rather than the onset, so that Onset Maximalism can be maintained.

bott.ling   Here, the [l] is in the onset, since a vowel follows; and in this case therefore, the prohibition on onset *[tl] clusters means the [t] is in the coda of the first syllable only.

2.

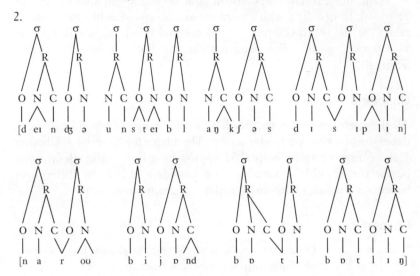

3. In this exercise, try to avoid making random lists of consonant clusters you can think of, and concentrate on narrowing down the possibilities using natural classes. For instance, in onset position, sonority rules out cases of liquids plus voiceless stops, so although [pl], [pr] are allowed, there are no initial clusters *[lp], *[rp], *[lt], *[rt], *[lk], *[rk]. Apparent medial exceptions would be *wallpaper, warpaint, alter, porter, alcohol, arcadia*. If the order voiceless stop plus liquid is permissible in onsets, it follows that this order must be ruled out in codas – and indeed, in English we find coda [lp], [lt], [lk], for instance, in *pulp, halt, milk*, but not *[pl], *[tl], *[kl], with ascending sonority; apparent medial exceptions are *apply, Atlantic, acclimatise*.

4. Again, these are just some indicative examples. English phonotactics generally forbid sequences of voiceless stop plus voiceless fricative, so *[ps] in onsets, but nonetheless we have *psittacosis, psyche*; similarly *[ts], but *tsetse* (fly). Likewise, English has no onsets with *[vl], but note the Russian name *Vlad*.

Chapter 10

1. There is no absolutely clear preference for the noun or the verb pattern in the adjectives in the list, although most can be interpreted as following the Noun Rule. *Surreal* seems to follow the Verb Rule, since it has final stress, which is not characteristic of nouns (leaving e.g. *machine, police* aside). However, *beautiful, scarlet* clearly follow the Noun Rule; both have heavy final syllables, so if following the verb pattern, they should carry final stress. *Sensible* probably falls into the same category. *Lovely* and *noisy* could follow either pattern, since their final syllables are short, meaning that stress would retract to the penultimate syllable in a verb, while the penult is the target for noun stress anyway. *High-pitched* follows the usual compound pattern, with initial stress. Can you think of other adjectives which might settle the issue?

2.

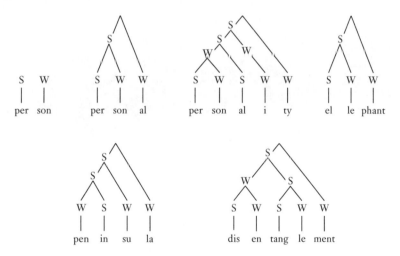

3. one iamb – *suppose, believe, machine*
   one trochee – *letter, open, answer*
   one dactyl – *cinema, enemy, quality*
   iamb plus trochee – these would be candidates for stress clashes, since the iamb has final stress, and the trochee, initial stress: the closest we can get would be compounds like *belief system, advance warning*.
   dactyl plus trochee – *phantasmagoric, paediatrician, multiplication*

4. The analysis here will depend very much on the poems you choose, and on how regular the rhythm is in each case. The brief examples worked out in the text should help; and you might find it useful to think

initially what a rhythm made up of a sequence of each foot type in isolation would sound like.

5. Citation forms (for SSBE – other accents will vary):

[aɪ ɛkspɛkt hiː haz gɒn tu miːt hɜː]
[hɛlən had ə bənɑːnə and ə bɹɛd keɪk]

Fast speech forms:
[aspɛktɪzgɒntəmiːtə]
[hɛlənadəbnɑːnəɹənəbɹɛgkeɪk]

Note multiple reduction of vowels to schwa; assimilation of place of articulation of the first stop to the second in the middle of *bread cake*; intrusive [r]; reduction of *he has* to *he's*; dropping of [h] in *had, her* and *he*.

References

Aitchison, Jean (1983), *The Articulate Mammal*, London: Hutchinson.

Archangeli, Diana and D. Terence Langendoen (eds) (1997), *Optimality Theory: An Overview*, Oxford: Blackwell.

Ball, Martin and Joan Rahilly (1999), *Phonetics: The Science of Speech*, London: Arnold.

Campbell, Lyle (1998), *Historical Linguistics*, Edinburgh University Press.

Carr, Philip (1993), *Phonology*, London: Macmillan.

Carr, Philip (1999), *English Phonetics and Phonology: An Introduction*, Oxford: Blackwell.

Catford, J. C. (1988), *A Practical Course in Phonetics*, Oxford: Oxford University Press.

Chambers, J. K. and Peter Trudgill (1980), *Dialectology*, Cambridge: Cambridge University Press.

Chomsky, Noam and Morris Halle (1968), *The Sound Pattern of English*, New York: Harper & Row.

Coulmas, Florian (1988), *The Writing Systems of the World*, Oxford: Blackwell.

Couper-Kuhlen, Elisabeth (1986), *An Introduction to English Prosody*, London: Arnold.

Cruttenden, Alan (1986), *Intonation*, Cambridge: Cambridge University Press.

Davenport, Mike and S. J. Hannahs (1998), *Introducing Phonetics and Phonology*, London: Arnold.

Durand, Jacques (1990), *Generative and Non-Linear Phonology*, London: Longman.

Fletcher, P. and B. MacWhinney (1994), *The Handbook of Child Language*, Oxford: Blackwell.

Fry, D. B. (1947), 'The frequency of occurrence of speech sounds in Southern English', *Archives néerlandaises de phonétique expérimentale*, 20: 103-6.

Giegerich, Heinz J. (1992), *English Phonology: An Introduction*, Cambridge: Cambridge University Press.

Graddol, David, Dick Leith and Joan Swann (1996), *English: History, Diversity and Change*, London: Routledge.

Gussenhoven, Carlos and Haike Jacobs (1998), *Understanding Phonology*, London: Arnold.

Hogg, Richard M. and C. B. McCully (1987), *Metrical Phonology: A Coursebook*, Cambridge: Cambridge University Press.

Hudson, Richard A. (1995), *Sociolinguistics* (2nd edn), Cambridge: Cambridge University Press.

International Phonetic Association (1999), *The Handbook of the International Phonetic Association*, Cambridge: Cambridge University Press.

Jones, Charles (ed.) (1997), *The Edinburgh History of the Scots Language*, Edinburgh: Edinburgh University Press.

Kager, René (1999), *Optimality Theory*, Cambridge: Cambridge University Press.

Kaisse, Ellen and Patricia Shaw (1985), 'On the theory of Lexical Phonology', *Phonology Yearbook*, 2: 1-30.

Katamba, Francis (1988), *An Introduction to Phonology*, London: Longman.

Ladd, D. Robert (1996), *Intonational Phonology*, Cambridge: Cambridge University Press.

Ladefoged, Peter (1993), A Course in Phonetics (3rd edn), New York: Harcourt, Brace, Jovanovitch.

Lass, Roger (1984), *Phonology*, Cambridge: Cambridge University Press.

Laver, John (1994), *Principle of Phonetics*, Cambridge: Cambridge University Press.

Pinker, Steven (1994), *The Language Instinct*, London: Penguin.

Roach, Peter (2001), *English Phonetics and Phonology: A Practical Course* (2nd edn), Cambridge: Cambridge University Press.

Sampson, Geoffrey (1985), *Writing Systems*, London: Hutchinson.

Spencer, Andrew (1996), *Phonology*, Oxford: Blackwell.

Tan, Ludwig (1998), 'The vowel system of Singapore English', Unpublished M.Phil. essay, Department of Linguistics, University of Cambridge.

Trask, R. L. (1996), *Historical Linguistics*, London: Arnold.

Trudgill, Peter (2000), *The Dialects of England* (2nd edn), Oxford: Blackwell.

Wells, J. C. (1982), *Accents of English* (3 vols), Cambridge: Cambridge University Press.

Wolfram, Walt and Natalie Schilling-Estes (1996), *American English: Dialects and Variation*, Oxford: Blackwell.

Index

Note: entries in **bold** give the place where the term is defined.